Country Houses
AND
Seaside Cottages
OF THE VICTORIAN ERA

CLUBHOUSE OF THE GREENWOOD LAKE ASSOCIATION.

VanCampen Taylor, Archt. Newark, N.J.

Country Houses
AND
Seaside Cottages
OF THE VICTORIAN ERA

WILLIAM T. COMSTOCK

DOVER PUBLICATIONS, INC., NEW YORK

NOTE
In this reprint edition, all plates have been reduced by 10 percent.
Readers should bear this in mind when dealing with any scales given on the plates.

Published in Canada by General Publishing Company, Ltd., 30 Lesmill Road, Don Mills, Toronto, Ontario.

Published in the United Kingdom by Constable and Company, Ltd., 10 Orange Street, London WC2H 7EG.

This Dover edition, first published in 1989, is a slightly revised republication of the work originally published by William T. Comstock, Architectural Publisher, New York, in 1883 under the title *American Cottages: Consisting of Forty-four Large Quarto Plates, Containing Original Designs of Medium and Low Cost Cottages, Seaside and Country Houses. Also, a Club House, Pavilion, School House, and a Small Seaside Chapel. Together with a Form of Specification for Cottages. All in the Latest Prevailing Styles, from the Drawings of a Number of Prominent Architects, Thus Securing a Great Variety of Plans and Diversity of Treatment, and Offering the Largest Opportunity for Selection.* The plates, unbacked in the original edition, are here reprinted on both verso and recto pages (Plate XIX remains unbacked). The "Form of Specification for Cottages," now following the plates, originally preceded Plate XXXII; it refers to that plate specifically.

Manufactured in the United States of America
Dover Publications, Inc., 31 East 2nd Street, Mineola, N.Y. 11501

Library of Congress Cataloging-in-Publication Data

Comstock, William T.
    [American cottages]
    Country houses and seaside cottages of the Victorian era / William T. Comstock.
        p.   cm.
    Reprint. Originally published: American cottages. New York : W.T. Comstock, 1883.
    ISBN 0-486-25972-2
    1. Country homes—United States. 2. Vacation homes—United States. 3. Seaside architecture—United States. 4. Architecture, Victorian—United States. I. Title.
NA7561.C65   1989
728'.0973—dc19   88-37187
                                                                              CIP

Architects ❋ and ❋ Designers

Who have Contributed to this Work:

BARLOW, ALFRED E.,	- - - - - -	New York.
BATES, WM. A.,	- - - - - -	"
DEWSON, EDWARD,	- - - - - -	"
GIFFORD, CHAS. A.,	- - - - - -	Newark, N. J.
HUNTER, JAS. D., JR.,	- - - - - -	New York.
HUSS, GEO. MARTIN,	- - - - - -	"
HALLETT, WM. T.,	- - - - - -	"
JANES, FRANKLIN H.,	- - - - -	Albany, N. Y.
KIMBALL & WISEDELL,	- - - - - -	New York.
POWELL, GEO. T.,	- - - - - -	"
PROVOOST, DAVID B.,	- - - - -	Elizabeth, N. J.
ROSSITER & WRIGHT,	- - - - -	New York.
SIBELL, H. GARDNER,	- - - - -	Brooklyn, N. Y.
STROUD, JAMES,	- - - - - -	New York.
TAYLOR, VAN CAMPEN,	- - - - - -	Newark, N. J.
TUTHILL, WM. B.,	- - - - - -	New York.
WARD, FRANK F.,	- - - - - -	"
WHITE, FRED. B.,	- - - - - -	Princeton, N. J.
WOLF, JOHN C.,	- - - - - -	New York.

LIST OF PLATES

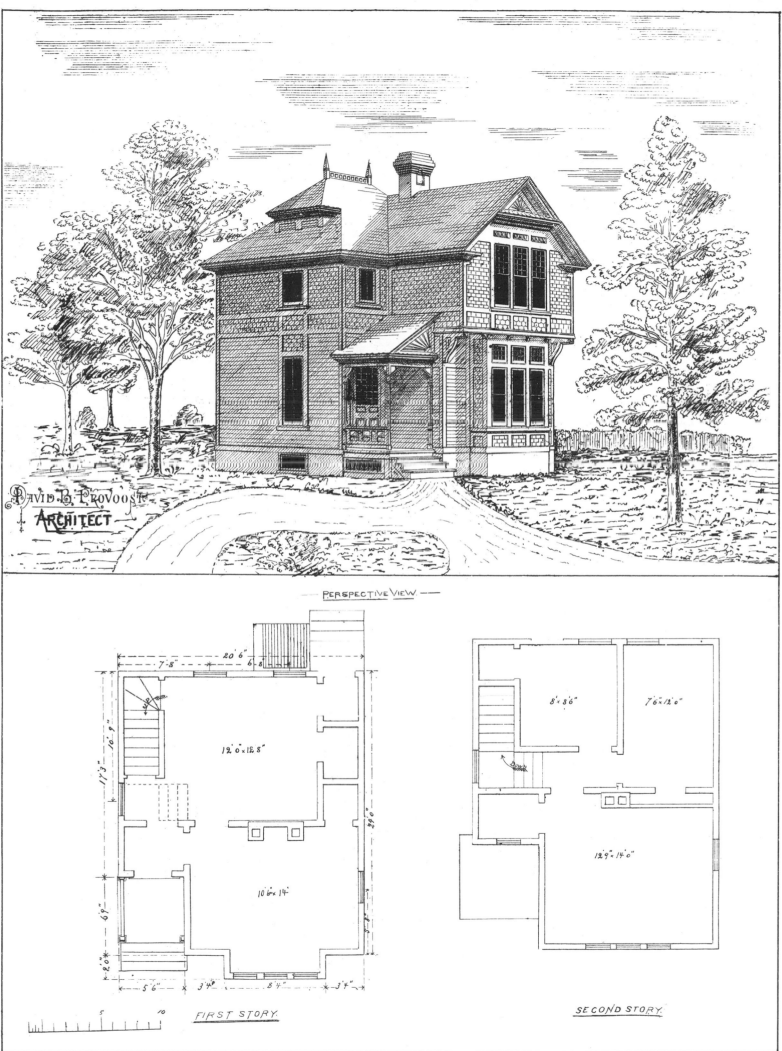

PERSPECTIVE VIEW.

FIRST STORY.

SECOND STORY.

— FRONT ELEVATION —

— SIDE ELEVATION —

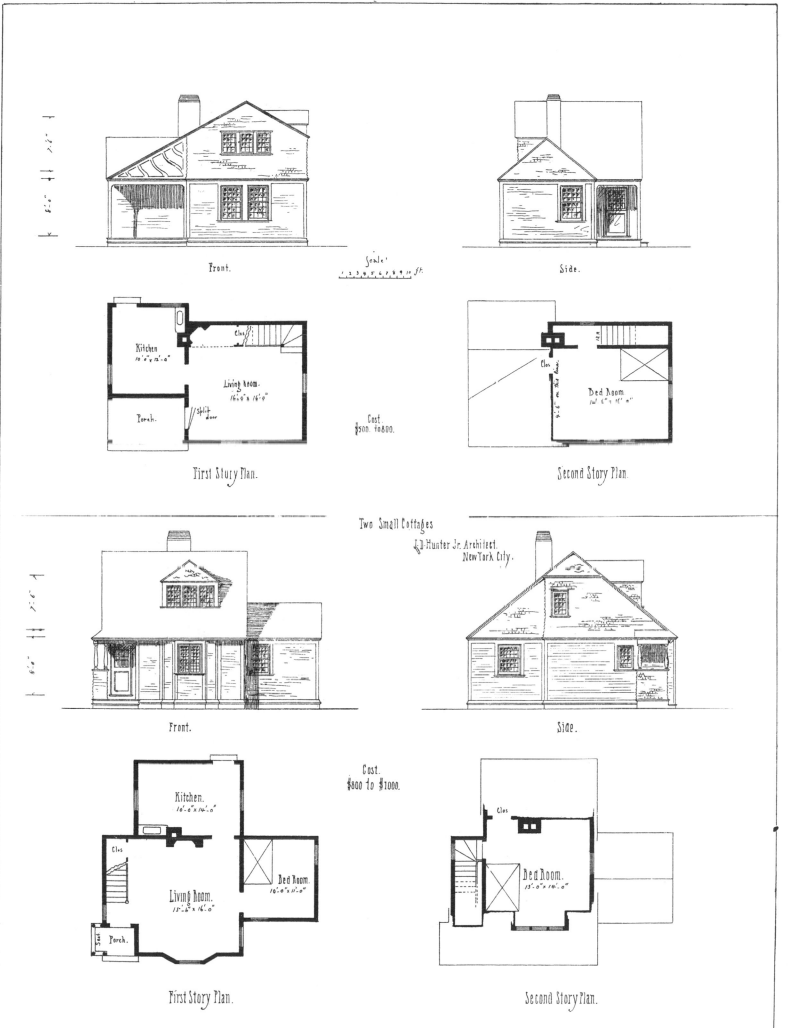

Front.

Scale:
1 2 3 4 5 6 7 8 9 10 ft.

Side.

Kitchen
10'-0" x 12'-0"

Clos.

Living Room.
16'-9" x 16'-0"

Porch.

Split door

Cost.
$500. to 800.

First Story Plan.

Clos.

Bed Room
10'-6" x 16'-0"

Second Story Plan.

Two Small Cottages
J. D. Hunter Jr. Architect.
New York City.

Front.

Side.

Kitchen.
10'-0" x 14'-0"

Clos.

Living Room.
15'-6" x 16'-0"

Bed Room.
10'-0" x 11'-0"

Porch.

Cost.
$800 to $1000.

Clos.

Bed Room.
13'-0" x 14'-0"

First Story Plan.

Second Story Plan.

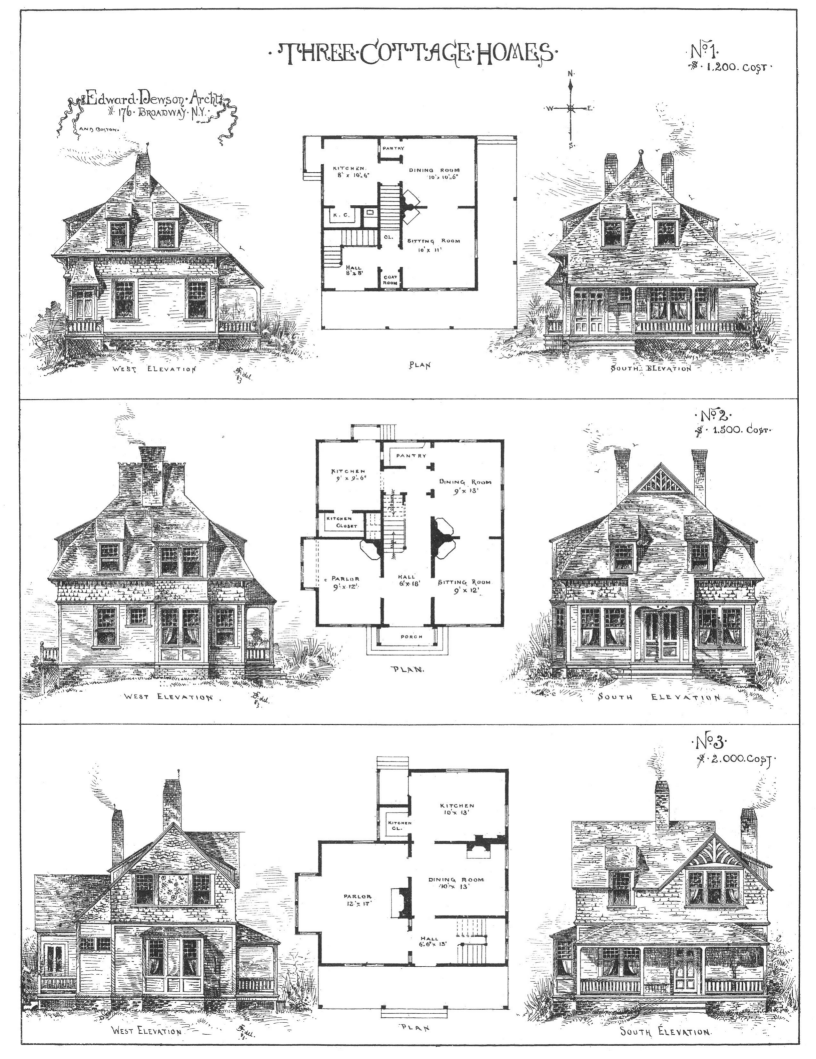

· THREE · COTTAGE · HOMES ·

№ 1.
$ · 1.200. COST ·

Edward · Dewson · Archt.
№ 176 · BROADWAY · N.Y.
AND BOSTON.

PANTRY
KITCHEN 8' x 10'.6"   DINING ROOM 10' x 10'.6"
K. C.
CL.   SITTING ROOM 10' x 11'
HALL 8' x 8'   COAT ROOM

WEST ELEVATION
PLAN
SOUTH ELEVATION

· № 2 ·
$ · 1.500. COST ·

PANTRY
KITCHEN 9' x 9'.6"   DINING ROOM 9' x 13'
KITCHEN CLOSET
PARLOR 9' x 12'   HALL 6' x 18'   SITTING ROOM 9' x 12'
PORCH

WEST ELEVATION.
PLAN.
SOUTH ELEVATION

· № 3 ·
$ · 2.000. COST ·

KITCHEN 10' x 13'
KITCHEN CL.
PARLOR 12' x 17'   DINING ROOM 10' x 13'
HALL 6'.6" x 13'

WEST ELEVATION
PLAN
SOUTH ELEVATION

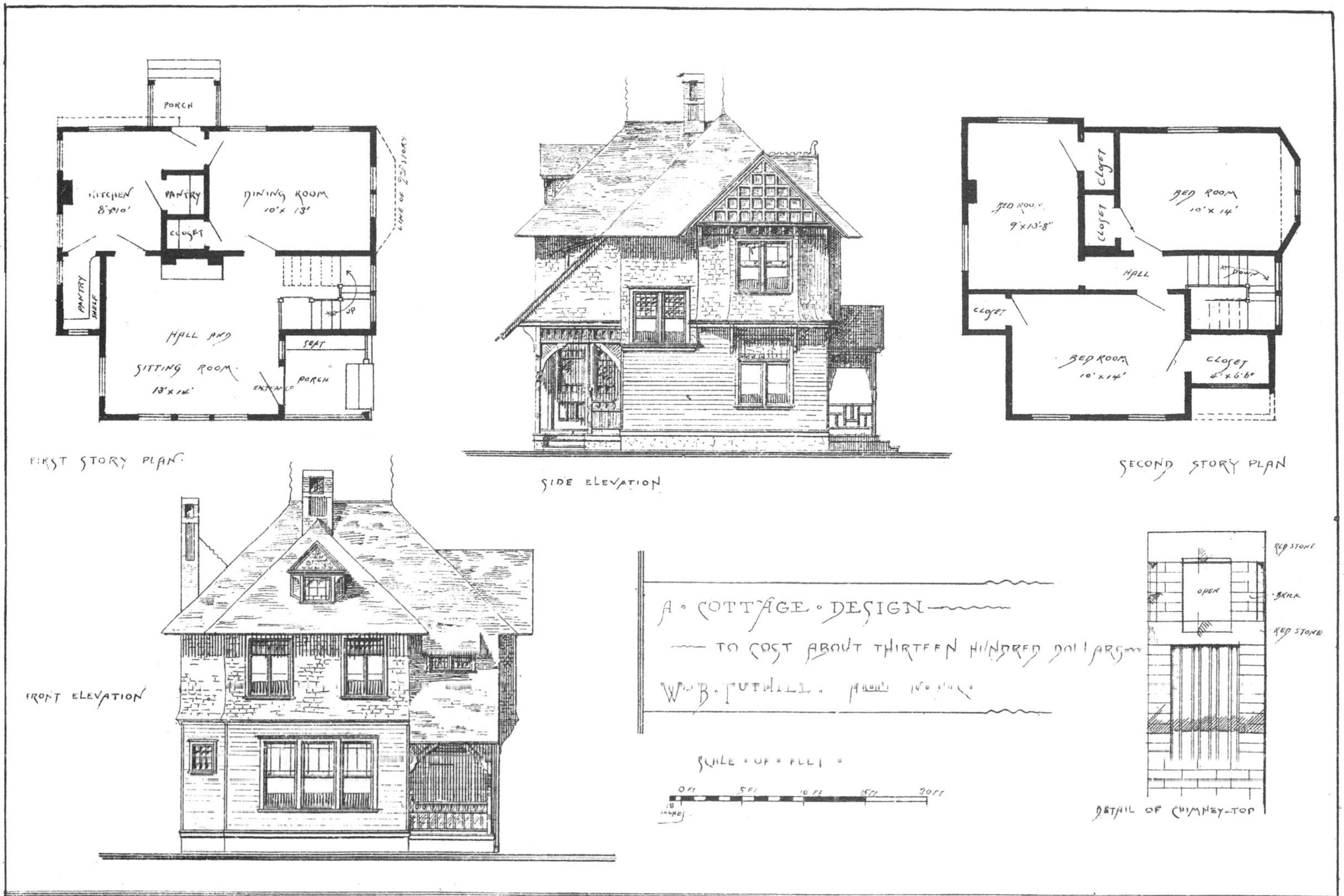

FIRST STORY PLAN

SIDE ELEVATION

SECOND STORY PLAN

FRONT ELEVATION

A · COTTAGE · DESIGN
— TO COST ABOUT THIRTEEN HUNDRED DOLLARS —
Wm B. Tuthill. Arch't N.Y.C.

SCALE OF FEET

DETAIL OF CHIMNEY-TOP

FRONT ELEVATION

SIDE ELEVATION

FIRST STORY PLAN

SECOND STORY PLAN

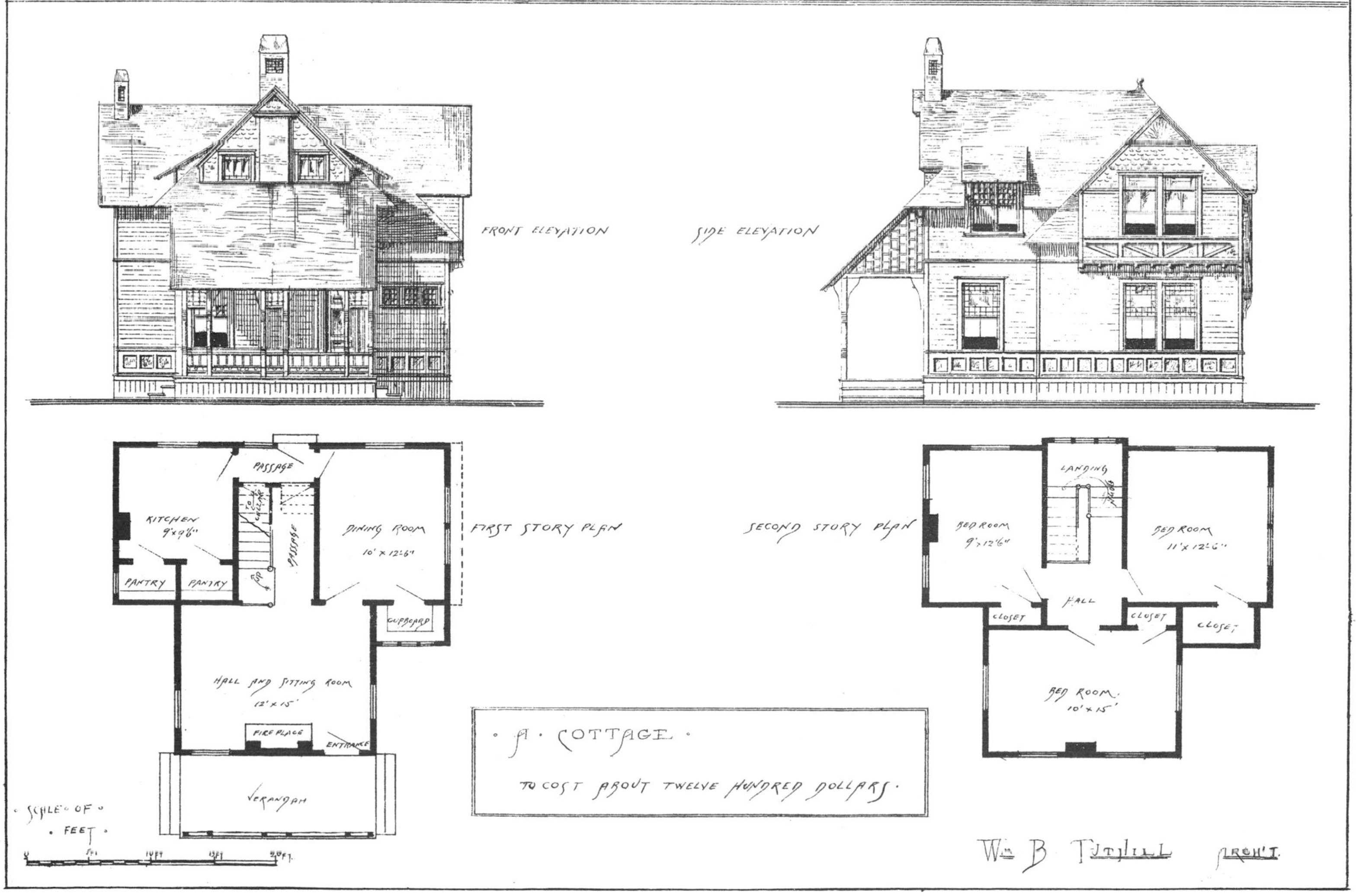

A · COTTAGE ·
TO COST ABOUT TWELVE HUNDRED DOLLARS.

SCALE OF FEET

Wm B. Tuthill Arch't

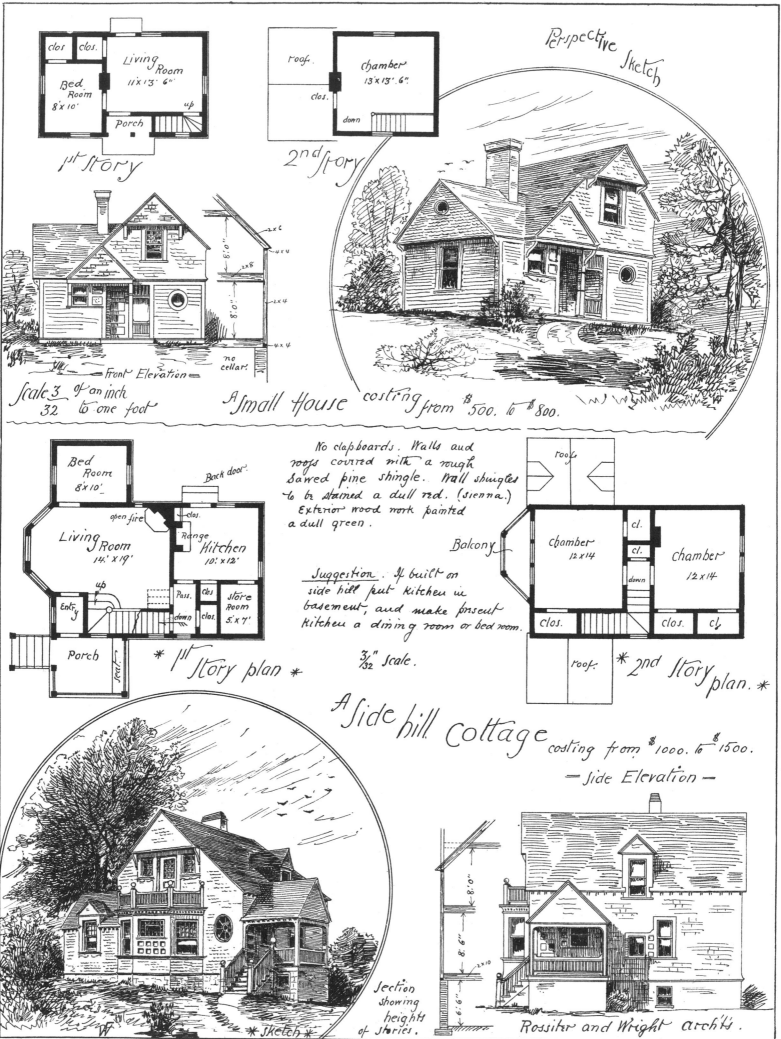

clos. | clos.

Living Room
11' x 13'. 6".

Bed Room
8' x 10'

up

Porch

1st Story

roof.

chamber
13' x 13'. 6".

clos.

down

2nd Story

Perspective Sketch

2 x 6

8'. 0"

4 x 4

2 x 8

8'. 0"

2 x 4

4 x 4

no cellar.

Front Elevation

Scale 3/32 of an inch to one foot

A Small House costing from $500. to $800.

Bed Room
8' x 10'

Back door.

open fire

clos.

Living Room
14'. x 19'

Range

Kitchen
10'. x 12'

Entry

up

Pass.

down

clos

clos.

Store Room
5.' x 7'

Porch

seat.

1st Story plan

No clapboards. Walls and roofs covered with a rough sawed pine shingle. Wall shingles to be stained a dull red. (sienna.) Exterior wood work painted a dull green.

Suggestion. If built on side hill put kitchen in basement, and make present kitchen a dining room or bed room.

3/32" Scale.

roof

Balcony

Chamber
12 x 14

cl.

cl.

down

Chamber
12 x 14

Clos.

clos.

cl.

roof.

2nd Story plan.

A Side hill Cottage costing from $1000. to $1500.

— Side Elevation —

8'. 0"

8'. 6"

6'. 6"

2 x 10

Section showing heights of stories.

* Sketch *

Rossiter and Wright arch'ts.

Front

Side

Sketch looking from rear.

Dining Room.
12'-0" x 17'-0"

Kitchen.
12'-0" x 15'-0"

Pantry.

Parlour.
11'-0" x 18'-6"

Hall
12'-0" x 12'-0"

Coat Clos.

Vestibule

Piazza 10'-0" wide.

Clos

Bed Room
12'-0" x 15'-6"

Bed Room
12'-0" x 13'-6"

Closet under Stairs

To Attic

Bay

Bed Room
11'-0" x 17'-0"

Hall
7'-6" x 12'-0"

Clos

Bath Room
6'-0" x 8'-6"

Clos

Scale

First Story.

James D Hunter Jr. Architect.
New York City.

Second Story

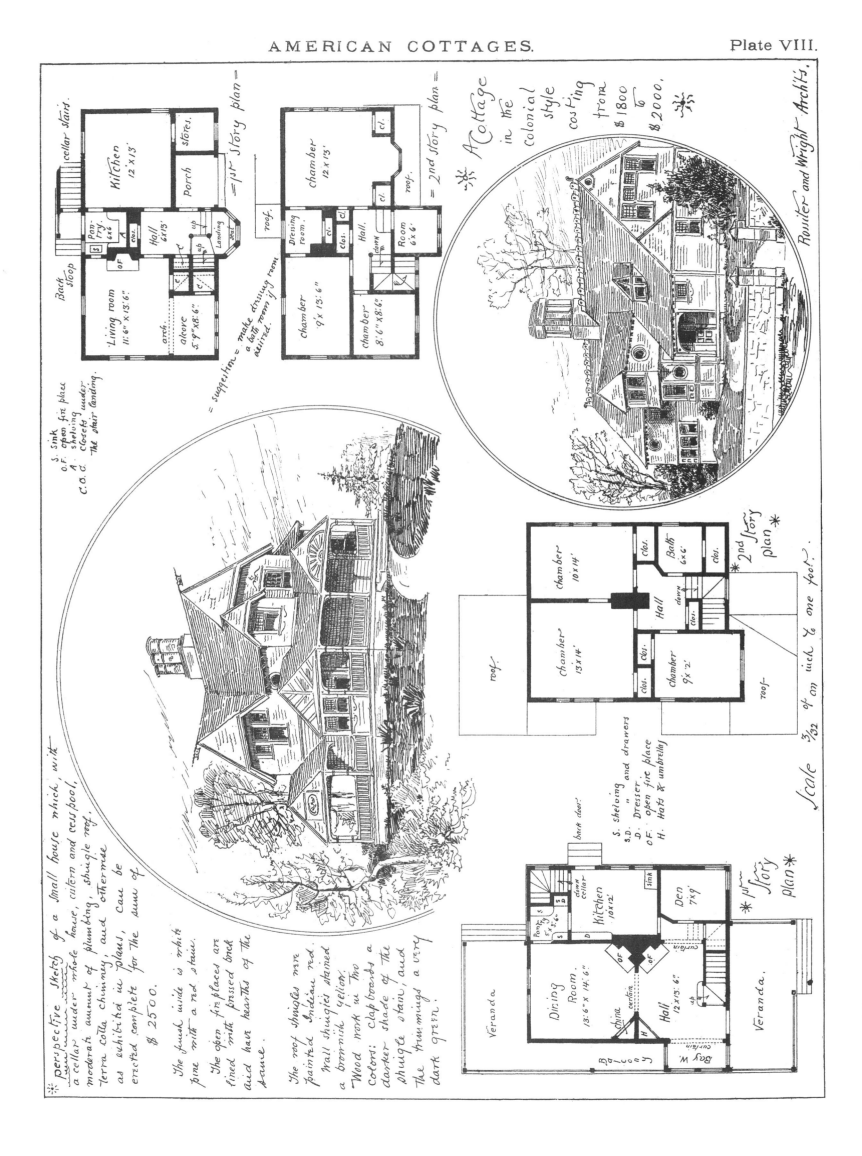

Rossiter and Wright, Arch'ts.

A Cottage in the colonial style costing from $1800 to $2000.

= 1st story plan =

= 2nd story plan =

= suggestion = make dressing room a bath room if desired. The stair landing.

S. sink
O.F. open fire place
A. shelving
C.O.G. closets under

1st story plan (top left):
- Back stoop
- cellar stairs
- Kitchen 12' x 13'
- Pantry 6 x 6
- clos.
- Hall 6' x 15'
- Porch
- stores.
- Living room 11' 6" x 13' 6"
- alcove 5' 9" x 8' 6"
- arch.
- up
- Landing
- seat

2nd story plan (top middle):
- roof.
- chamber 12' x 13'
- cl.
- Dressing room.
- clos.
- Hall.
- Room 6 x 6
- down
- chamber 9' x 13' 6"
- chamber 8' 6" x 8' 6"

2nd story plan (right):
- roof.
- chamber 10' x 14'
- clos.
- Bath 6 x 6'
- chamber 13' x 14'
- Hall
- clos.
- chamber 9' x 2'
- down
- roof.

1st story plan (bottom right):
- Veranda.
- Dining Room 13' 6" x 14' 6"
- china
- curtain
- Pantry 5 x 5' 6"
- down cellar
- Kitchen 10 x 12'
- sink
- Hall 12' x 15' 6"
- Den 7 x 9'
- Veranda.
- Bay W.

Scale 3/32 of an inch to one foot.

S. shelving and drawers
S.D. Dresser
D. Dresser
O.F. open fire place
H. Hats & umbrellas

perspective sketch of a small house which, with a cellar under whole house, cistern and cesspool, moderate amount of plumbing, shingle roof, terra cotta chimney, and otherwise as exhibited in plans, can be erected complete for the sum of $2500.

The finish inside is white pine with a red stain.

The open fireplaces are lined with pressed brick and have hearths of the same.

The roof shingles are painted Indian red. Wall shingles stained a brownish yellow. Wood work in two colors; clapboards a darker shade of the shingle stain, and the trimmings a very dark green.

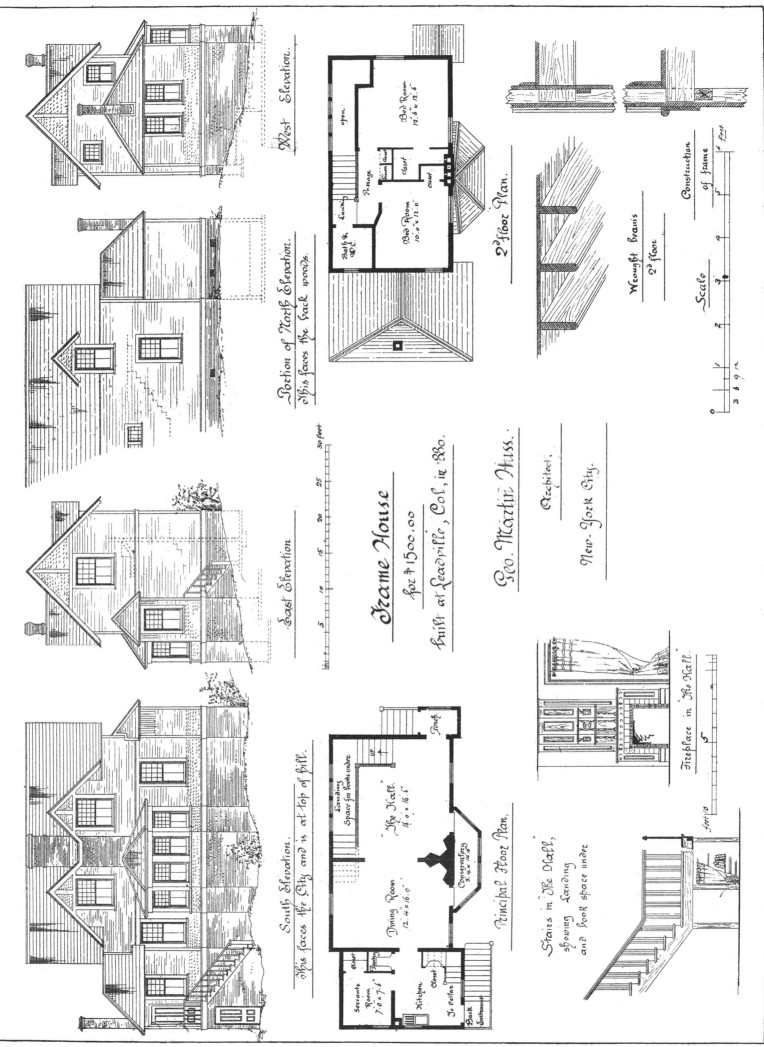

West Elevation.

Portion of North Elevation.
This faces the back woods.

East Elevation.

South Elevation.
This faces the City and is at top of hill.

2d Floor Plan.

Bed Room
12'.6" x 12'.6"

Bed Room
10'.0" x 12'.0"

Bath & W.C.

open

Passage

Linen Closet

closet

closet

Laundry

Construction of frame.

Wrought beams.
2d Floor.

Scale

Frame House
for $1500.00
Built at Leadville, Col., in 1880.

Geo. Martin Huss.

Architect,

New-York City.

Principal Floor Plan.

"The Hall"
15'.0" x 16'.6"

Dining Room
12'.4" x 16'.0"

Conservatory
5'.4" x 14'.0"

Porch

up

Landing
Space for Books under

Servant's Room
7'.0" x 7'.6"

Kitchen

closet

closet

Pantry

To cellar

Back Entrance

Stairs in "The Hall,"
showing Landing
and book space under.

Fireplace in "The Hall."

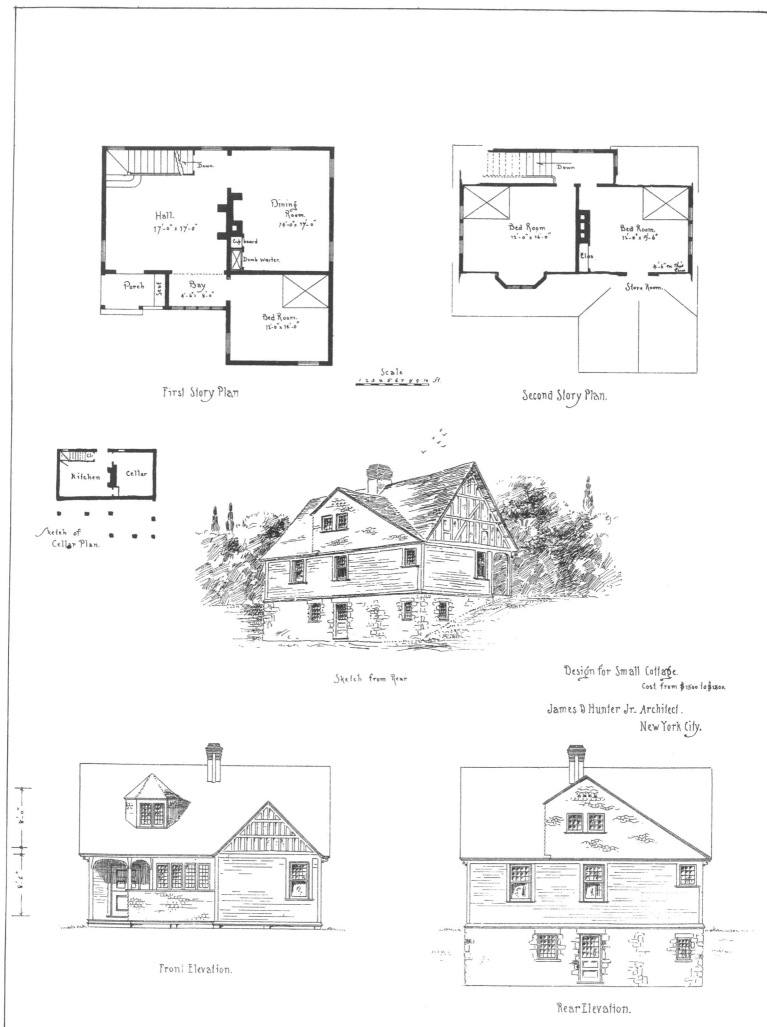

Hall.
17'-0" x 17'-0"

Dining Room.
14'-0" x 17'-0"

Cupboard
Dumb Waiter.

Porch   Seat   Bay
4'-6" x 8'-0"

Bed Room.
12'-0" x 14'-0"

First Story Plan

Down.

Bed Room
12'-0" x 16'-0"

Bed Room.
12'-0" x 19'-6"

Clos.

4'-6" on this floor

Store Room.

Second Story Plan.

Scale
1 2 3 4 5 6 7 8 9 10 ft.

Cl.

Kitchen   Cellar

Sketch of Cellar Plan.

Sketch from Rear

Design for Small Cottage.
Cost from $1500 to $1800.

James D Hunter Jr. Architect.
New York City.

Front Elevation.

Rear Elevation.

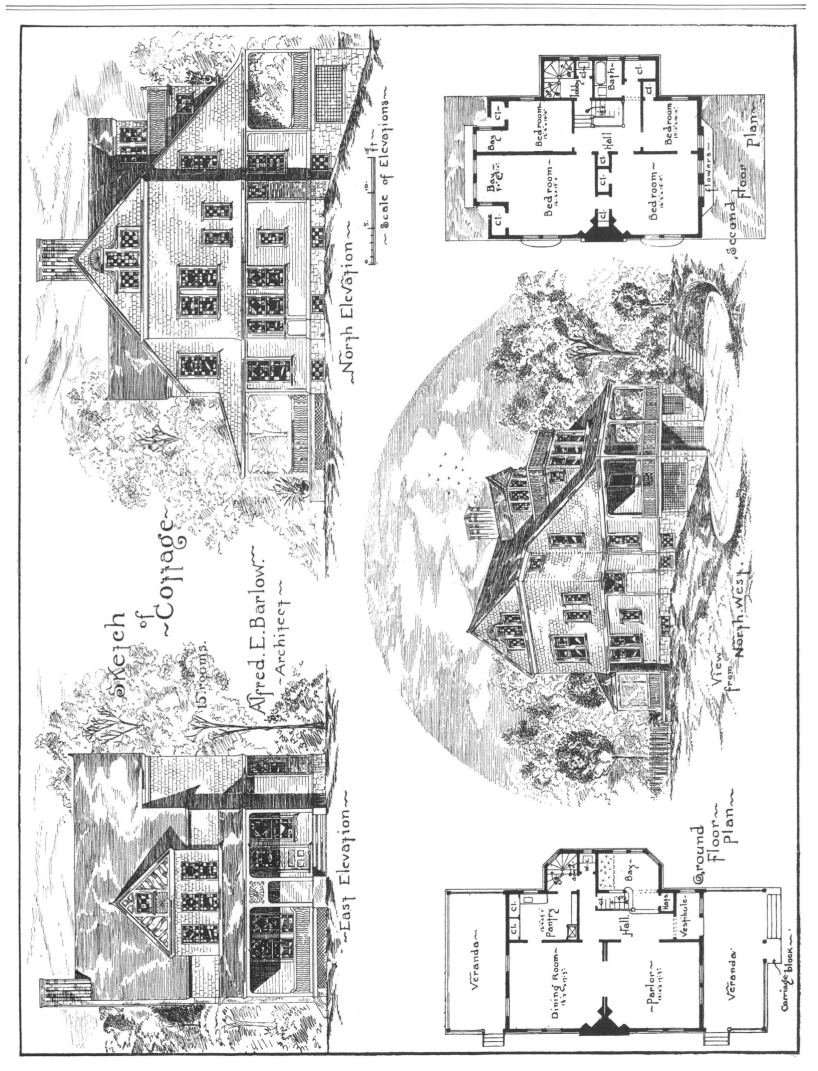

~North Elevation~

~Scale of Elevations~

~Second Floor Plan~

~Sketch of ~Cottage~

15 rooms.

~Alfred E. Barlow~
~Architect~

~East Elevation~

~View from North West.~

~Ground Floor Plan~

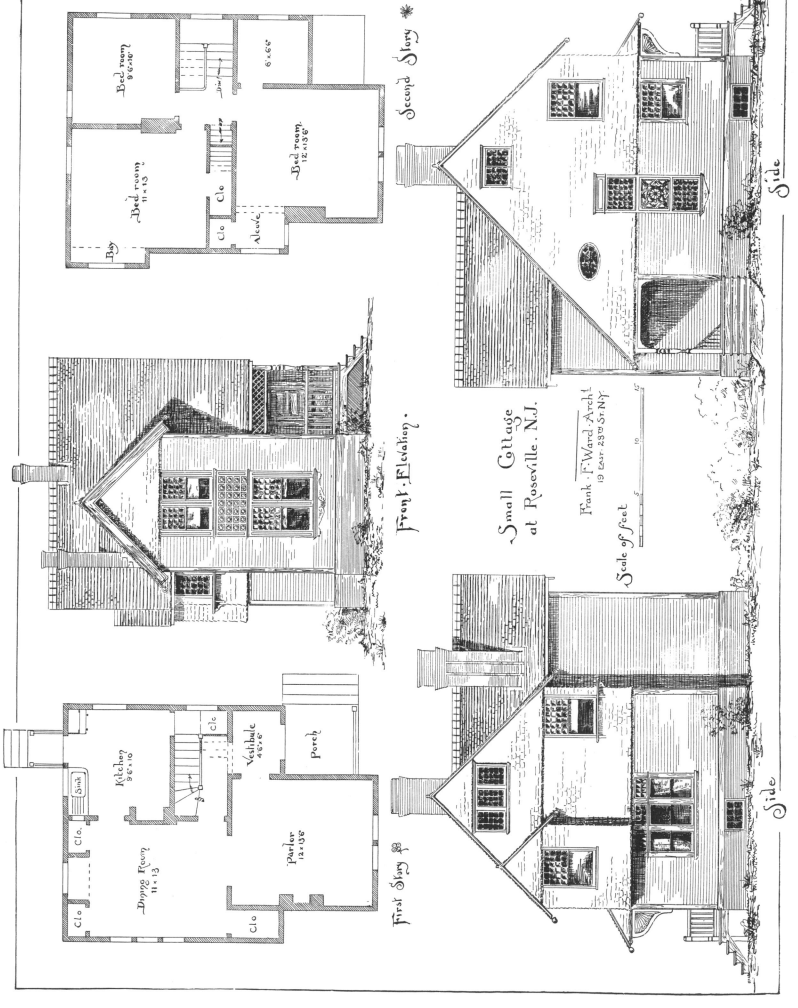

Bed room 9'6"x10'

6'x6'6"

Bed room 11 x 13

Clo

Clo

Bed room. 12 x 13'6"

Clo

Alcove

Bay

Second Story

Kitchen 9'6"x10

Sink

Clo.

Clo

Clo

Dining Room 11 x 13

Vestibule 4'6"x6'

Parlor 12 x 13'6"

Porch

Clo

First Story

Front Elevation.

Small Cottage at Roseville. N.J.

Frank·F·Ward·Arch.t 19 East 28th St. N.Y.

Scale of feet

5   10   15

Side.

Side.

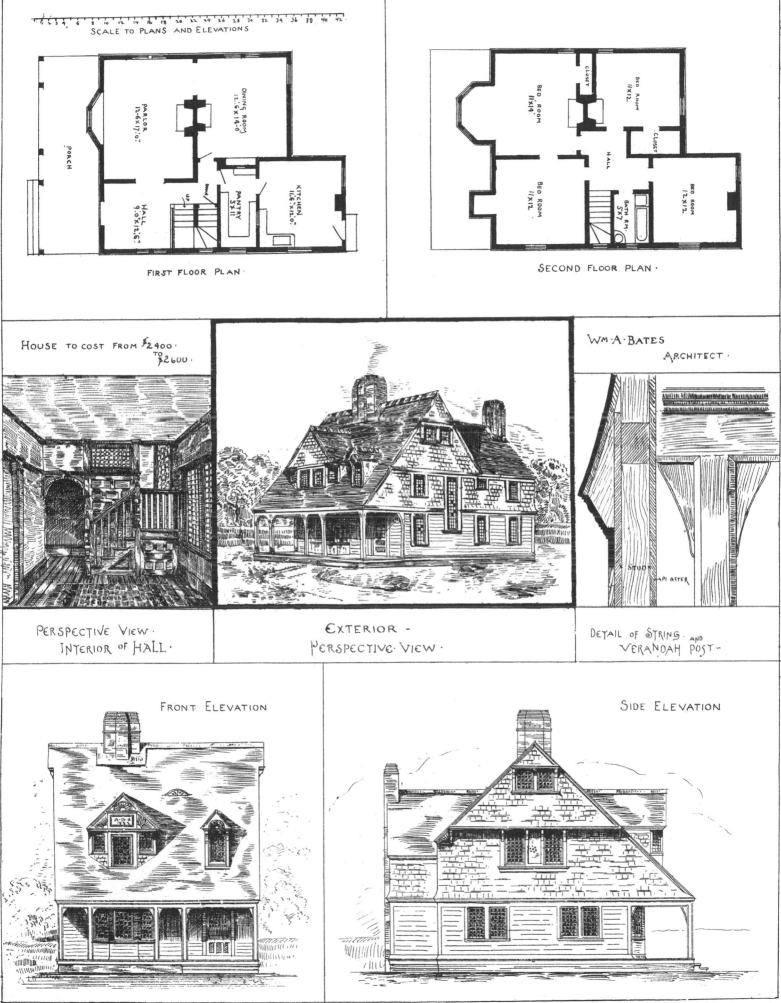

SCALE TO PLANS AND ELEVATIONS

FIRST FLOOR PLAN.

SECOND FLOOR PLAN.

HOUSE TO COST FROM $2400. TO $2600.

WM. A. BATES ARCHITECT.

PERSPECTIVE VIEW. INTERIOR OF HALL.

EXTERIOR - PERSPECTIVE VIEW.

DETAIL OF STRING. AND VERANDAH POST.

FRONT ELEVATION

SIDE ELEVATION

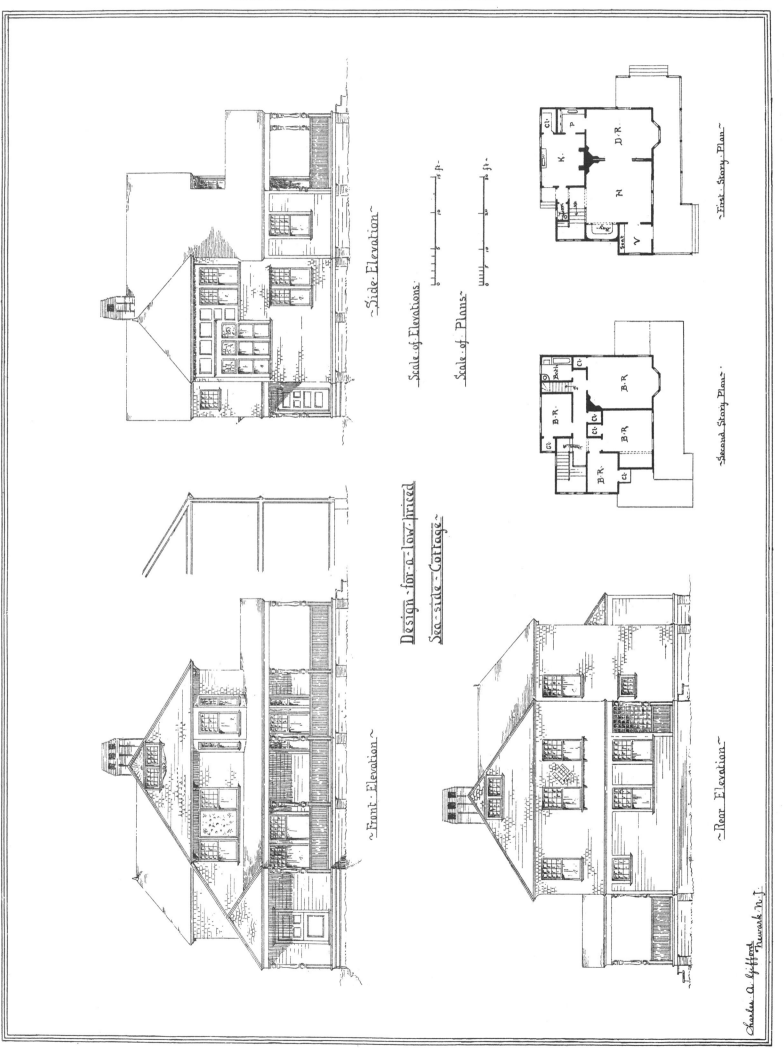

~Side·Elevation~

~First·Story·Plan~

~Second·Story·Plan~

Scale·of·Elevations~

Scale·of·Plans~

Design·for·a·low·priced
Sea·side·Cottage

~Front·Elevation~

~Rear·Elevation~

Charles A. Gifford
Newark N.J.

A $3000.00 Cottage
·Fred B. White·
··Architect···
~~ PRINCETON·N·J·

Perspective Sketch

$3500. Cottage

Rossiter and Wright
Architects.

<u>Description</u>. Cellar with cistern under kitchen. Portable hot air furnace. Drainage to two cesspools. Approved plumbing. Two good rooms in attic besides tank and trunk room. Finish inside white pine stained throughout. Exterior finish; slate roof; terra-cotta cristing and finials; shingles stained light red; other wood work painted in two shades of redish grey or russet. Exact cost of whole, complete as above described $3500 in vicinity of New York.

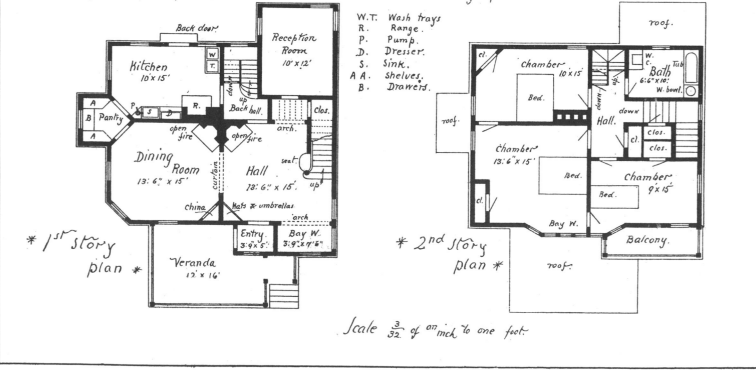

W.T. Wash trays
R. Range.
P. Pump.
D. Dresser.
S. Sink.
A A. Shelves.
B. Drawers.

* 1st story plan *

* 2nd story plan *

Scale 3/32 of an inch to one foot.

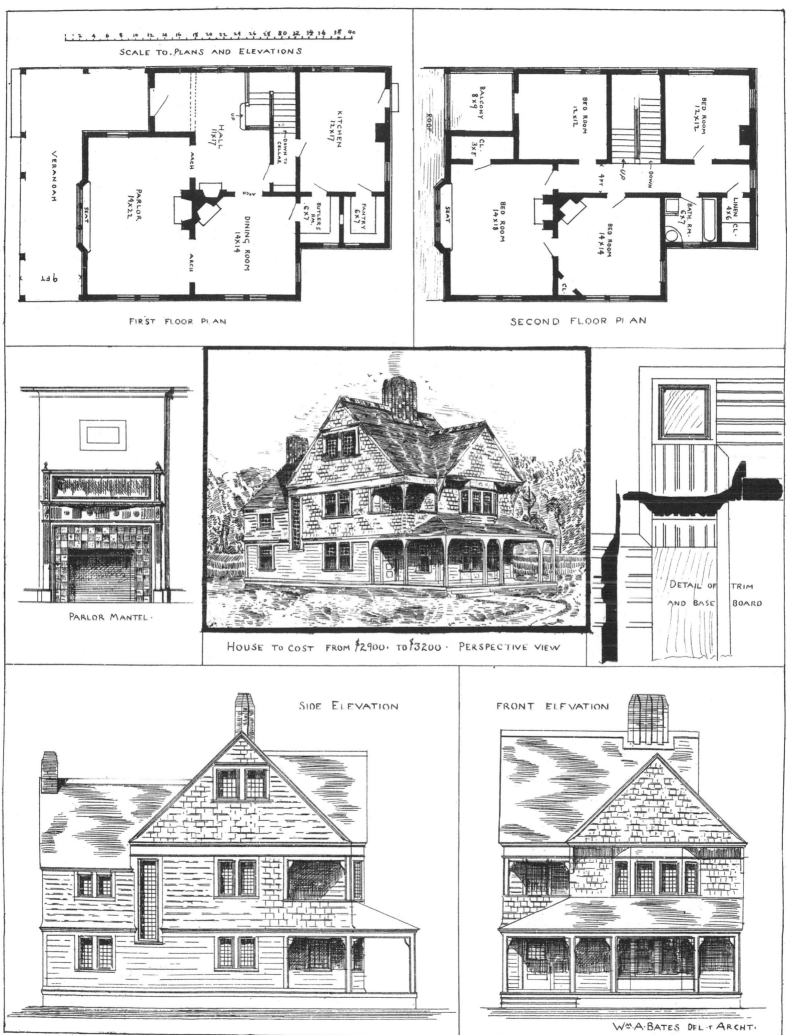

SCALE TO PLANS AND ELEVATIONS

FIRST FLOOR PLAN

SECOND FLOOR PLAN

PARLOR MANTEL.

HOUSE TO COST FROM $2900. TO $3200. PERSPECTIVE VIEW

DETAIL OF TRIM AND BASE BOARD

SIDE ELEVATION

FRONT ELEVATION

WM. A. BATES DEL. T ARCHT.

GROUND FLOOR. CHAMBER FLOOR. ATTIC FLOOR.

SCALE OF MEASUREMENTS FOR PLANS

FRANKLIN H JANES · ARCHITECT ·
· ALBANY · N.Y.

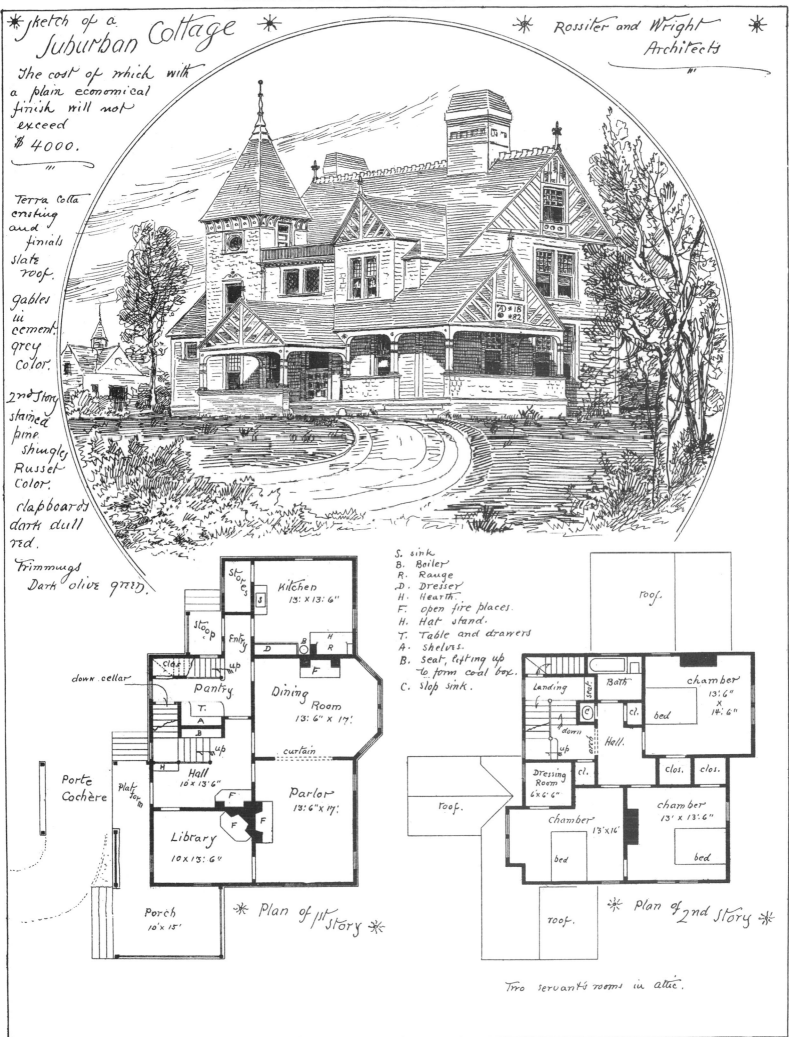

Sketch of a *Suburban Cottage*

The cost of which with a plain economical finish will not exceed $4000.

Terra cotta cresting and finials slate roof.

Gables in cement grey color.

2nd Story stained pine shingles Russet color.

clapboards dark dull red.

Trimmings Dark olive green.

Rossiter and Wright Architects

S. sink
B. Boiler
R. Range
D. Dresser
H. Hearth
F. open fire places.
H. Hat stand.
T. Table and drawers
A. Shelves.
B. Seat, lifting up to form coal box.
C. Slop sink.

Plan of 1st Story

- Stores
- Kitchen 13' X 13'6"
- Stoop
- Entry
- clos.
- down cellar
- Pantry
- Dining Room 13'6" X 17'
- curtain
- Porte Cochère
- Platform
- Hall 10' X 13'6"
- Parlor 13'6" X 17'
- Library 10 X 13'6"
- Porch 10' X 15'

Plan of 2nd Story

- roof.
- Landing
- Bath
- chamber 13'6" X 14'6"
- bed
- cl.
- down
- up
- porch
- Hall
- Dressing Room 6' X 6'6"
- cl.
- clos.
- clos.
- roof.
- Chamber 13' X 16'
- bed
- chamber 13' X 13'6"
- bed
- roof.

Two servant's rooms in attic.

Pantry. W.c.
Cl.
Dining room
20 x 17.
Hall
27 x 17.
Bay.
Veranda.
Entrance Hall
15 x 13.
Veranda.
Porch.
Ground Floor Plan.

Bedroom
16 x 14.
Cl.
Bath.
Corridor.
Bedroom
16 x 13.
Bedroom
15 x 14.
Bedroom.
Bedroom
15 x 18.
balcony.
Second Floor Plan.
Cost $5200.

Mountain~ Homes~

Kitchen.
13 x 13.
1st Story of Lodge.
Porch. Pantry.
Cl.
Hall. Parlor.
18 x 14.
Dining room
17 x 13.
Veranda.
~Ground Floor Plan~
Cost $2800.

Alfred E. Barlow.
Architect.
Cl. Cl.
B.r.
10 x 10-6.
B.
Hall.
B.r.
15-6 x 13.
Cl.
B.r.
15 x 14.
B.r.
9 x 11-6.
cl. cl.
balcony.
Second Floor Plan.

Plate XXI.   AMERICAN COTTAGES.

FIRST STORY PLANS

Houses for Hon. John Kelly, on Ave. St. Nicholas.

W. YORK.

JAMES STROUD - ARCHITECT. N.Y.

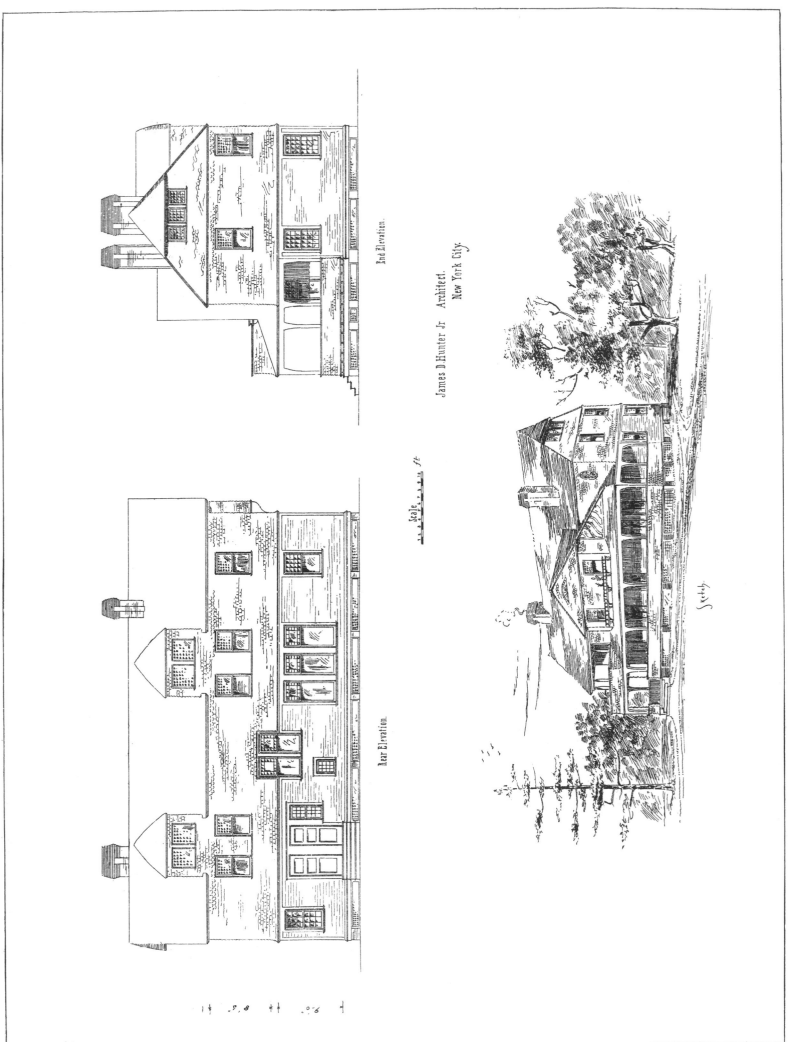

End Elevation.

Rear Elevation.

James D. Hunter Jr   Architect.
New York City.

Scale ___ ft

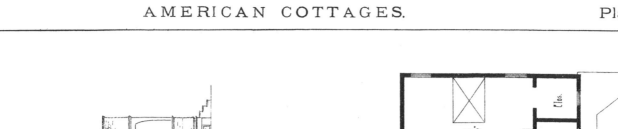

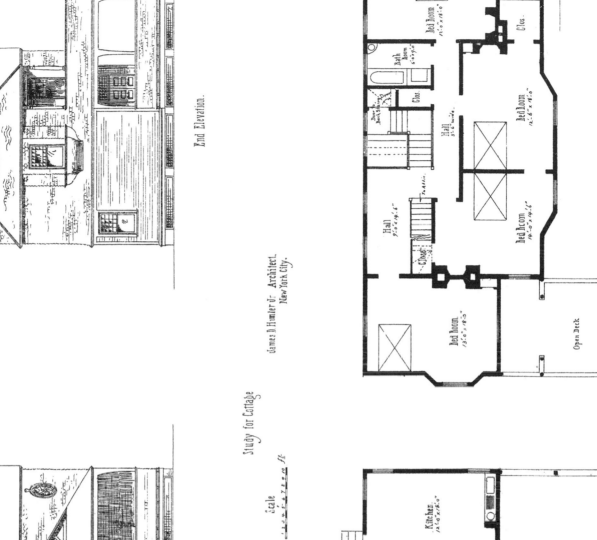

End Elevation.

Front Elevation.

Study for Cottage

Scale

James D. Hunter Jr. Architect.
New York City.

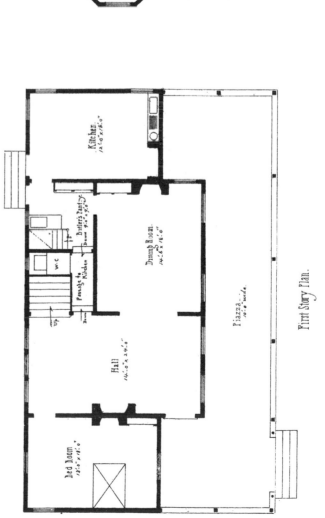

Second Story Plan.

First Story Plan.

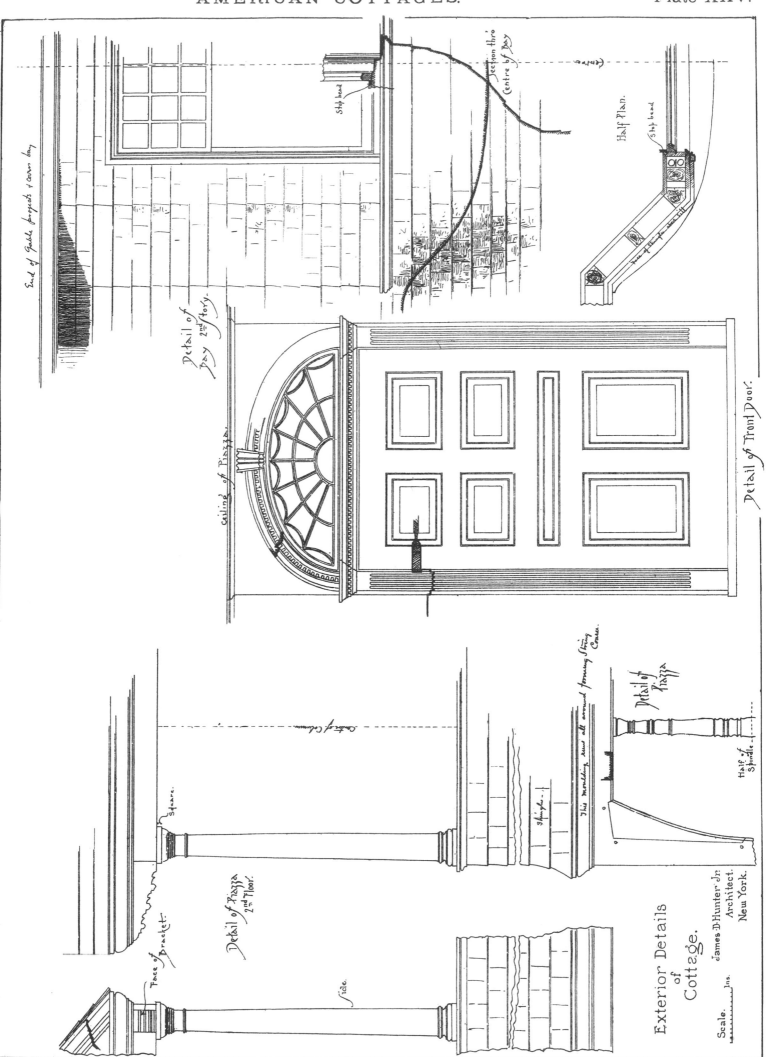

End of Gable projects 4 corner bay

Stop head

Section thro (centre of Bay)

Half Plan.

Stop head

Detail of Bay 2nd Story.

Ceiling of Piazza.

Detail of Front Door.

Out of Column.

Square.

Detail of Piazza 2nd Floor.

Shingles.

This moulding runs all around forming String Course.

Detail of Piazza

Half of Spindle

Face of Bracket.

Side.

Exterior Details of Cottage.

Scale. Ins.

James D. Hunter Jr. Architect. New York.

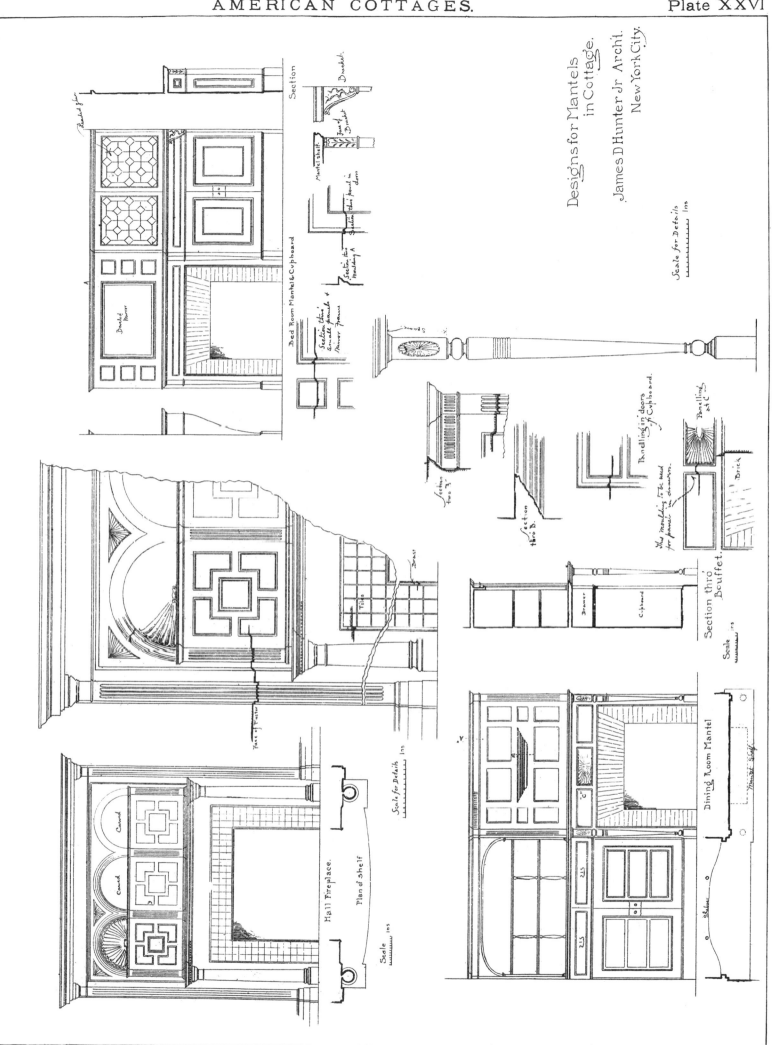

Designs for Mantels
in Cottage.

James D Hunter Jr Archt.
New York City.

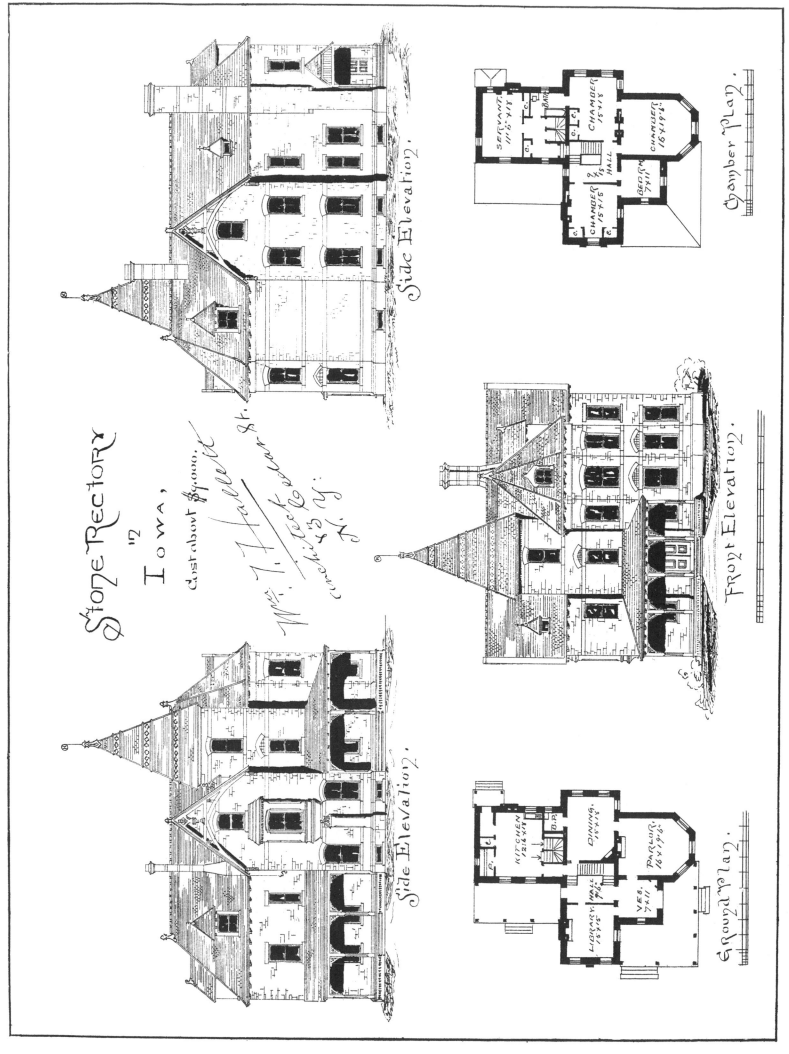

Side Elevation.

Chamber Plan.

Front Elevation.

Side Elevation.

Ground Plan.

Stone Rectory
" Iowa,
cost about $9,000.

Wm. T. Halsey
architect 43 solar St.
N. Y.

CHAMBER PLAN:
SERVANT. 11'6"x18'
CHAMBER 15'x18'
CHAMBER 16'x19'6"
BED RM. 7'x11'
CHAMBER 15'x15'
HALL

GROUND PLAN:
KITCHEN 12'6"x14'
DINING 15'x18'
PARLOR 16'x19'6"
LIBRARY 15'x15'
HALL
VES. 7'x11'

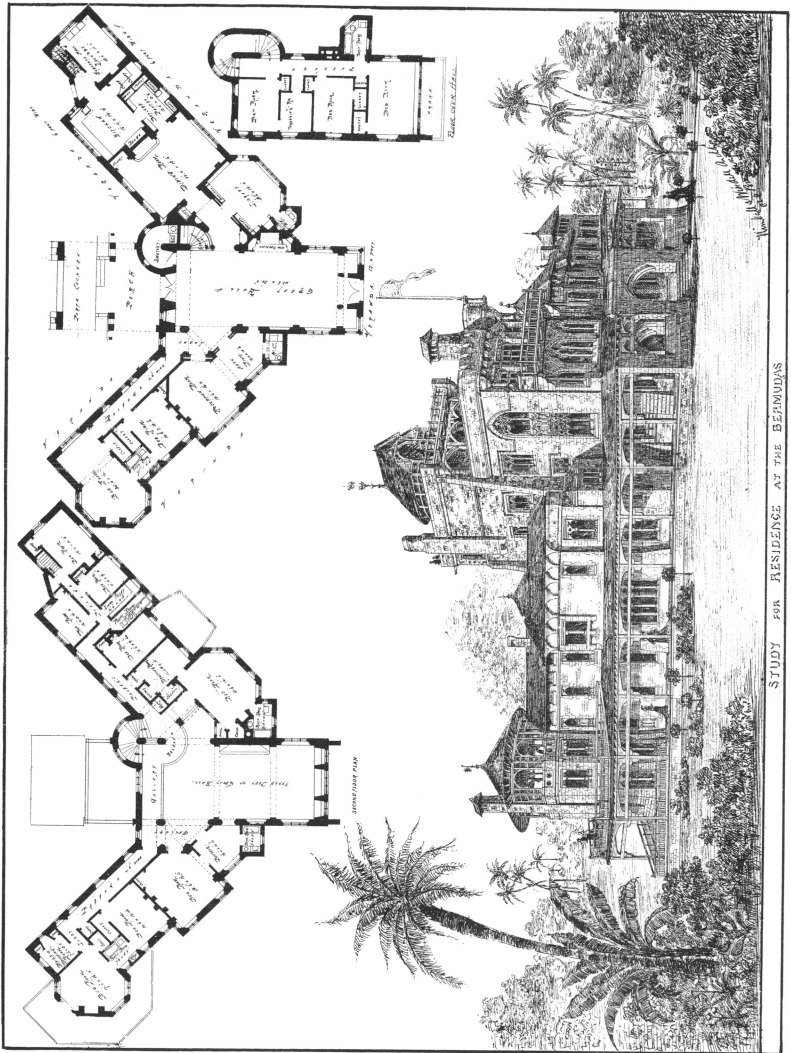

STUDY FOR RESIDENCE AT THE BERMUDAS.

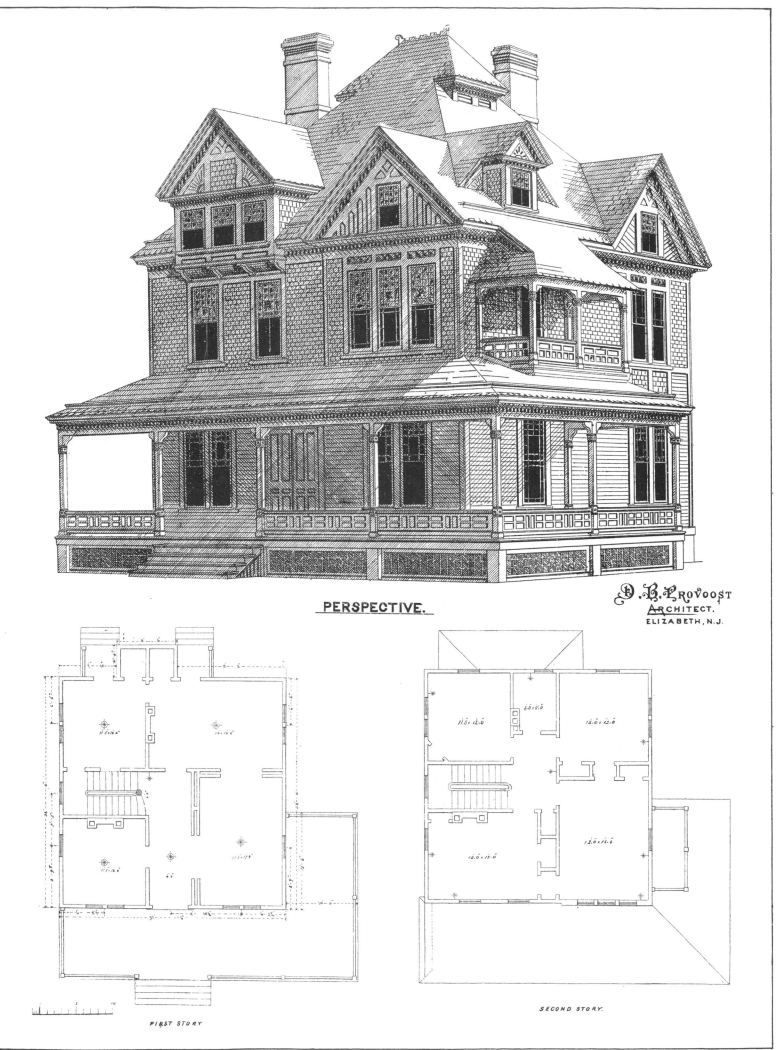

PERSPECTIVE.

O. B. Provoost
ARCHITECT.
ELIZABETH, N.J.

FIRST STORY

SECOND STORY.

FRONT ELEVATION

SIDE ELEVATION

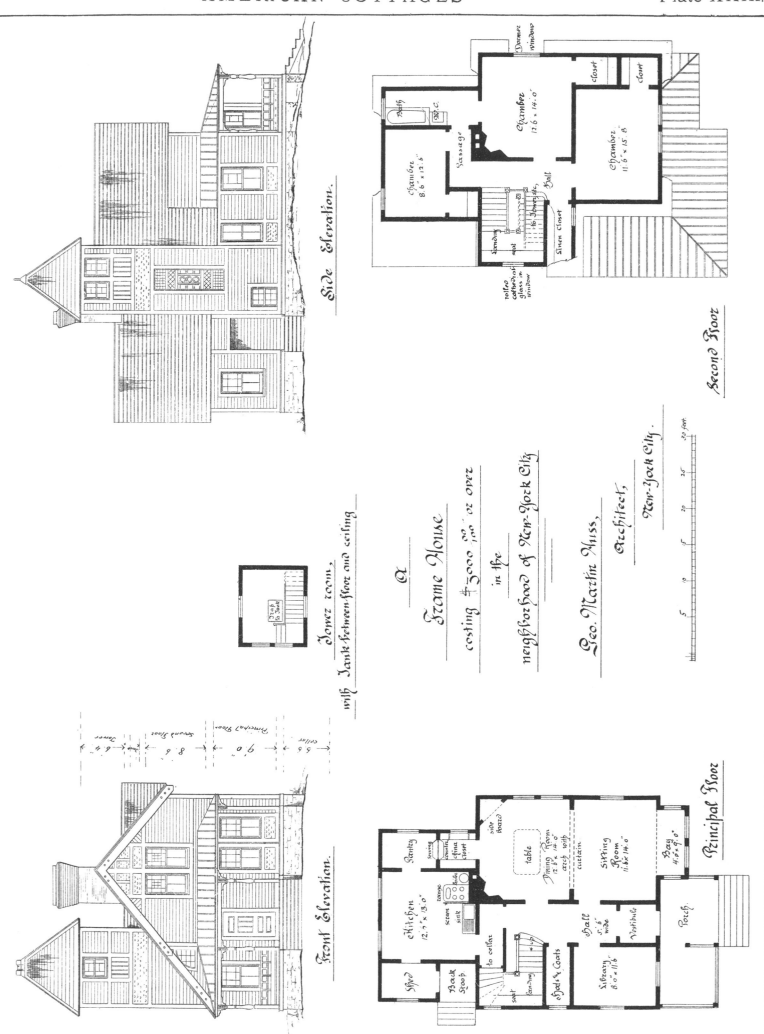

Side Elevation.

Second Floor

Front Elevation.

Tower room,
with Tank between floor and ceiling

A
Frame House
costing $3000 ⁰⁰ or over
in the
neighborhood of New-York City

Geo. Martin Huss,
Architect,
New-York City.

Principal Floor

[See specifications following the plates section.]

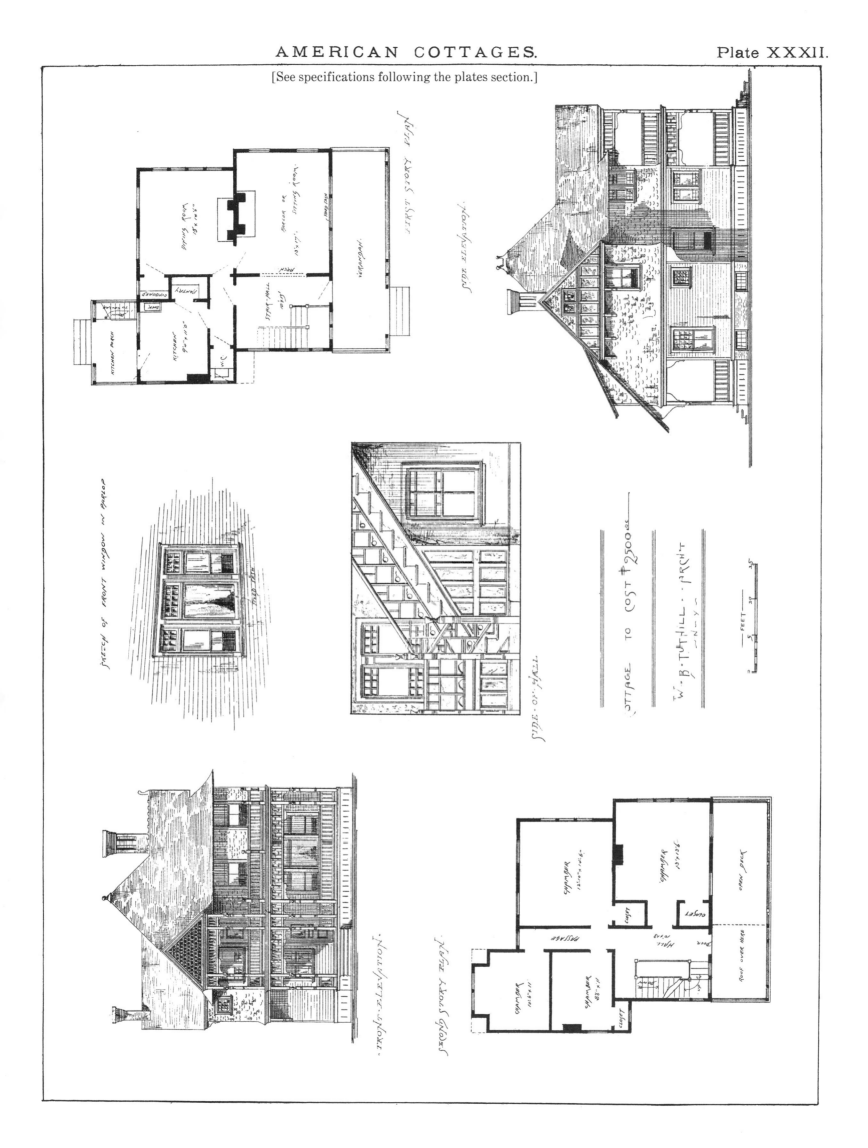

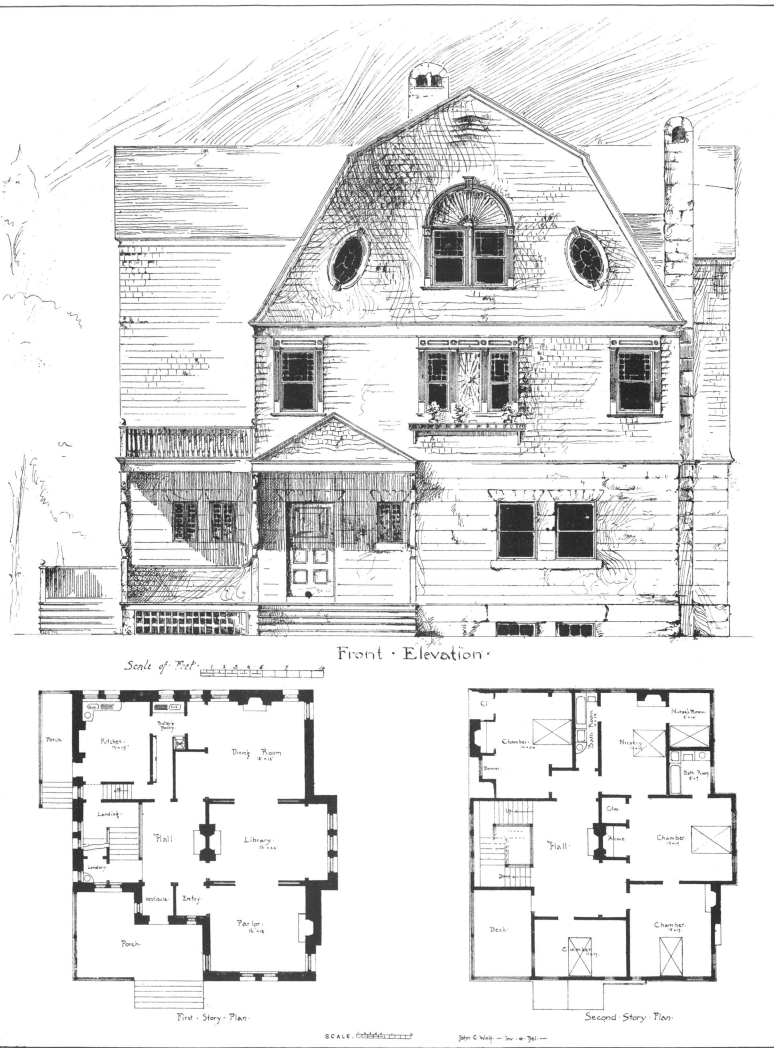

Front · Elevation ·

Scale of Feet.

First · Story · Plan ·

Second · Story · Plan ·

SCALE.

John C. Wolf — Inv · + · Del —

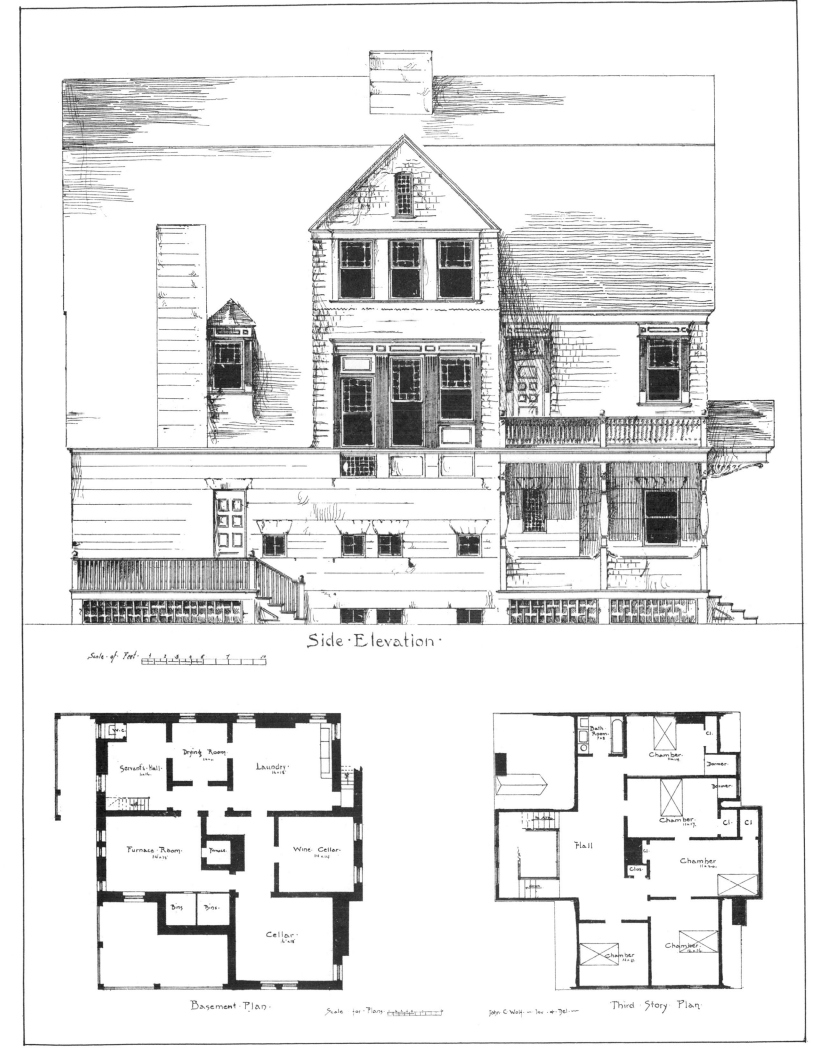

Side · Elevation ·

Scale · of · Feet ·

Basement · Plan ·

Scale · for · Plans ·

John · C · Wolf · — · Inv · & · Del ·—

Third · Story · Plan ·

Row of Brick Dwellings, English Style, American Plans.

Geo. T Powell
Arch't New York.

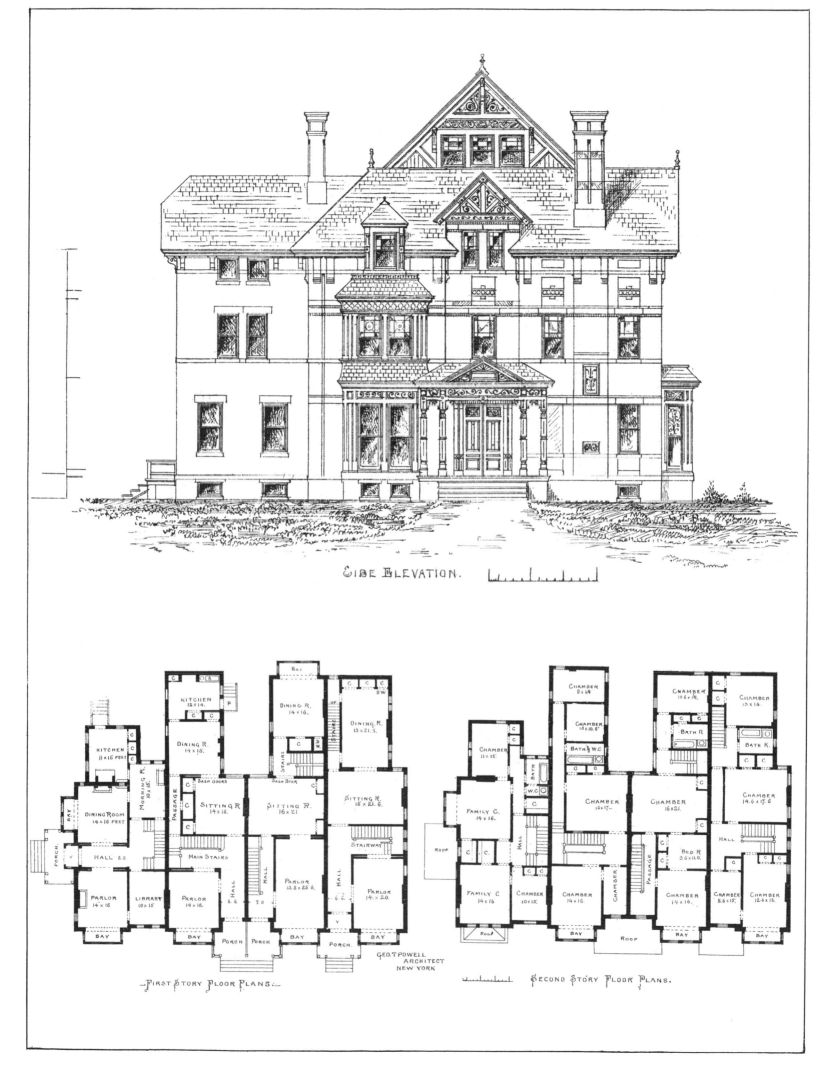

SIDE ELEVATION.

GEO. T. POWELL
ARCHITECT
NEW YORK

FIRST STORY FLOOR PLANS.

SECOND STORY FLOOR PLANS.

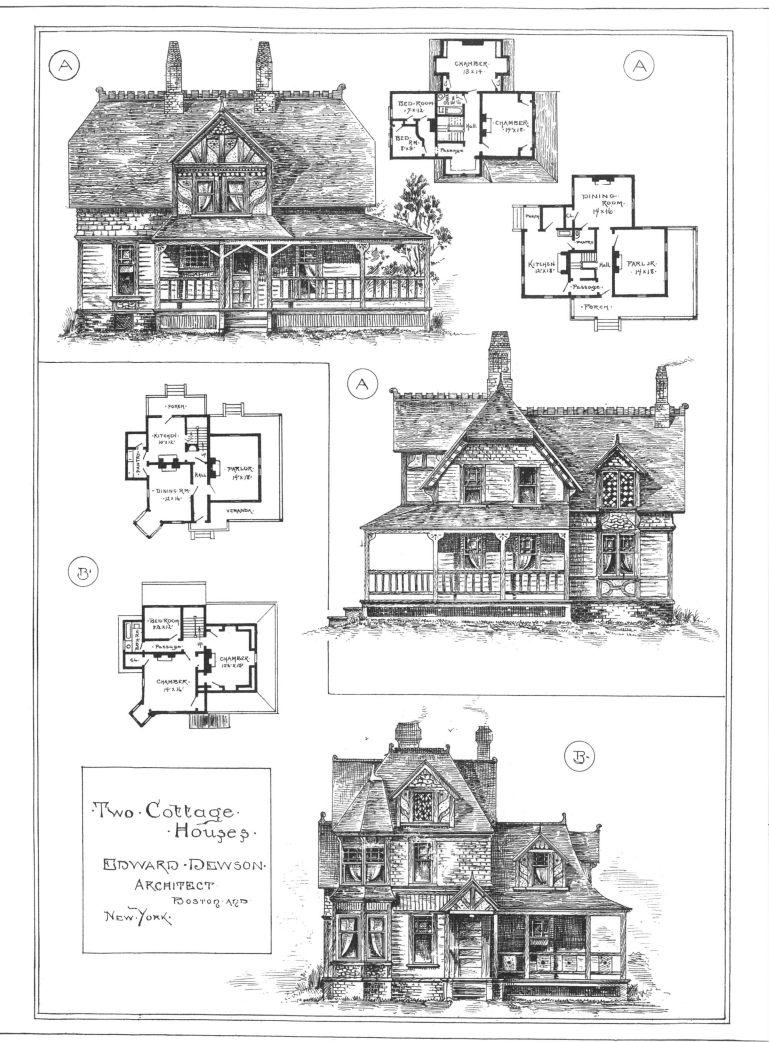

·Two·Cottage·
Houses·

EDWARD·DEWSON·
ARCHITECT·
BOSTON·AND·
NEW·YORK·

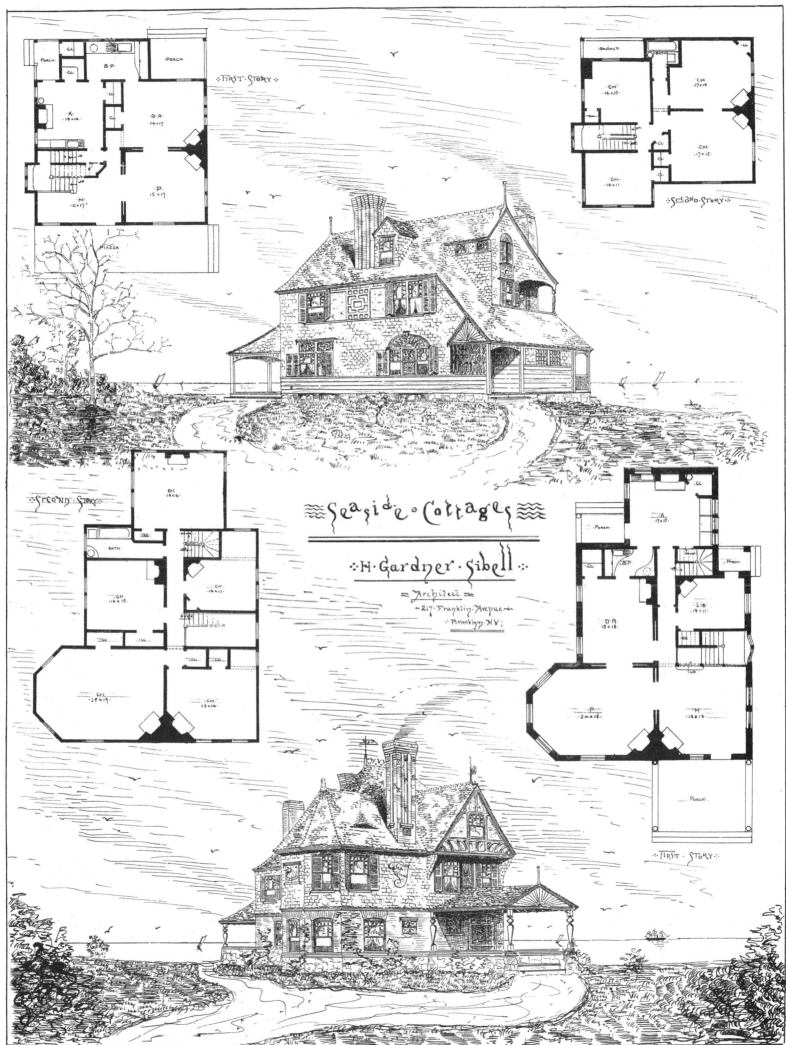

Seaside Cottages

H. Gardner Sibell

Architect
217 Franklin Avenue
Brooklyn N.Y.

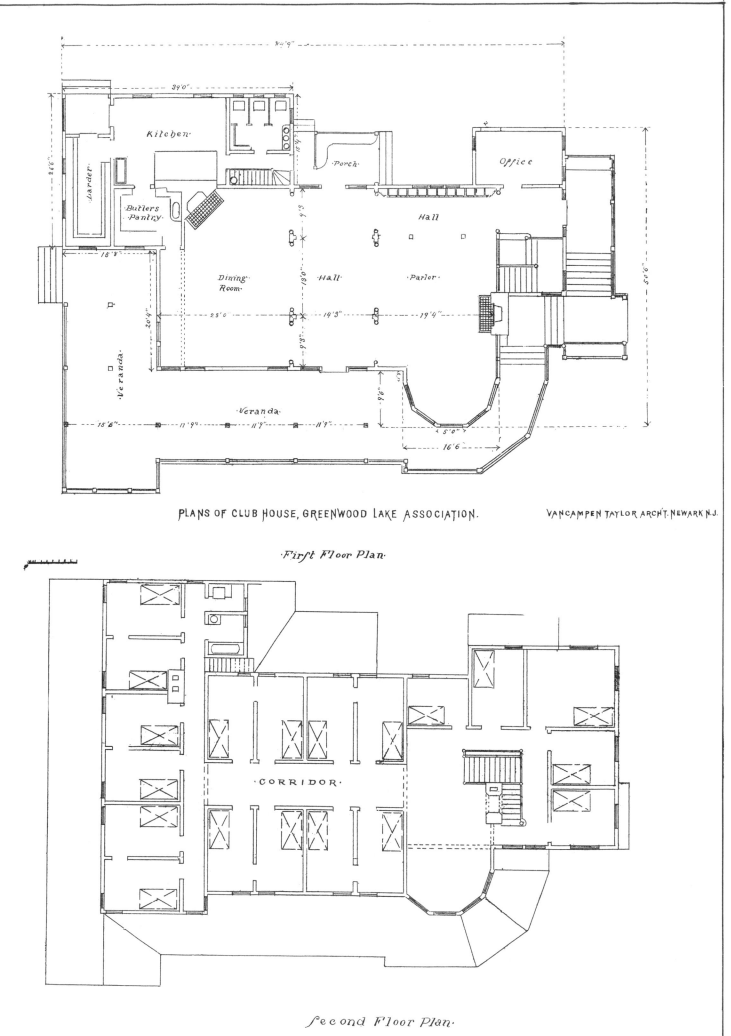

PLANS OF CLUB HOUSE, GREENWOOD LAKE ASSOCIATION.

VANCAMPEN TAYLOR ARCH'T. NEWARK N.J.

First Floor Plan.

Second Floor Plan.

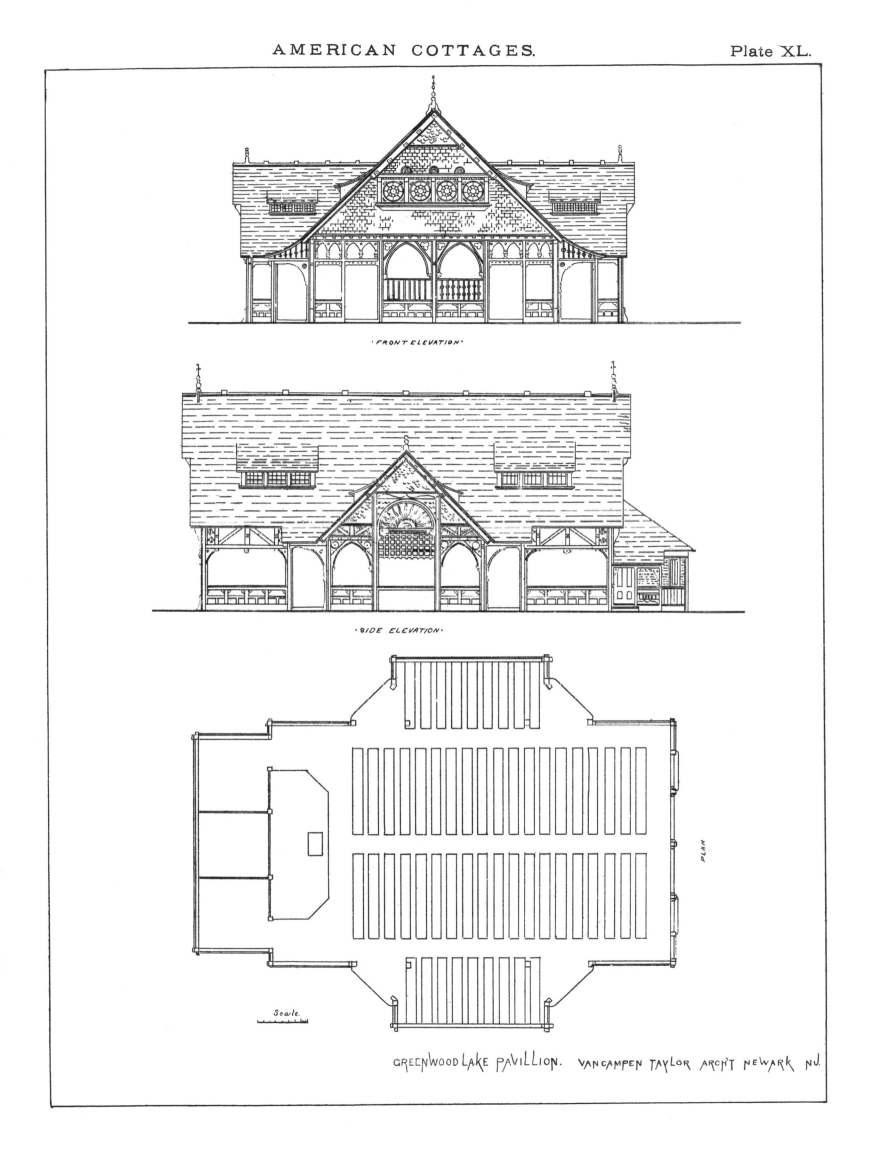

·FRONT ELEVATION·

·SIDE ELEVATION·

PLAN

Scale.

GREENWOOD LAKE PAVILLION.   VAN CAMPEN TAYLOR ARCH'T NEWARK N.J.

WEST DUBUQUE, IOWA :

PRELIMINARY STUDY FOR SCHOOL HOUSE : VIEW FROM ROAD. KIMBALL & WISEDELL ARCHTS N.Y.

Perspective Sketch

Ground Plan.

Seating capacity 200.

Bible or Infant Class. 10'x11' sliding doors

Baptistry 6'x14' Curtain Platform 6'x14' Pulpit door

Bible Class 10'x11'

Aisle 4'0" wide

Vestibule

Porch

Plastr. Plastr. Plastr. Wood.

Sketch of Interior.

Design for a

✳ Baptist Chapel ✳

at Long Branch N.J.

Rossiter and Wright, Architects.
149 B'way N.Y.C.

Scale of feet.
2 4 6 8   16

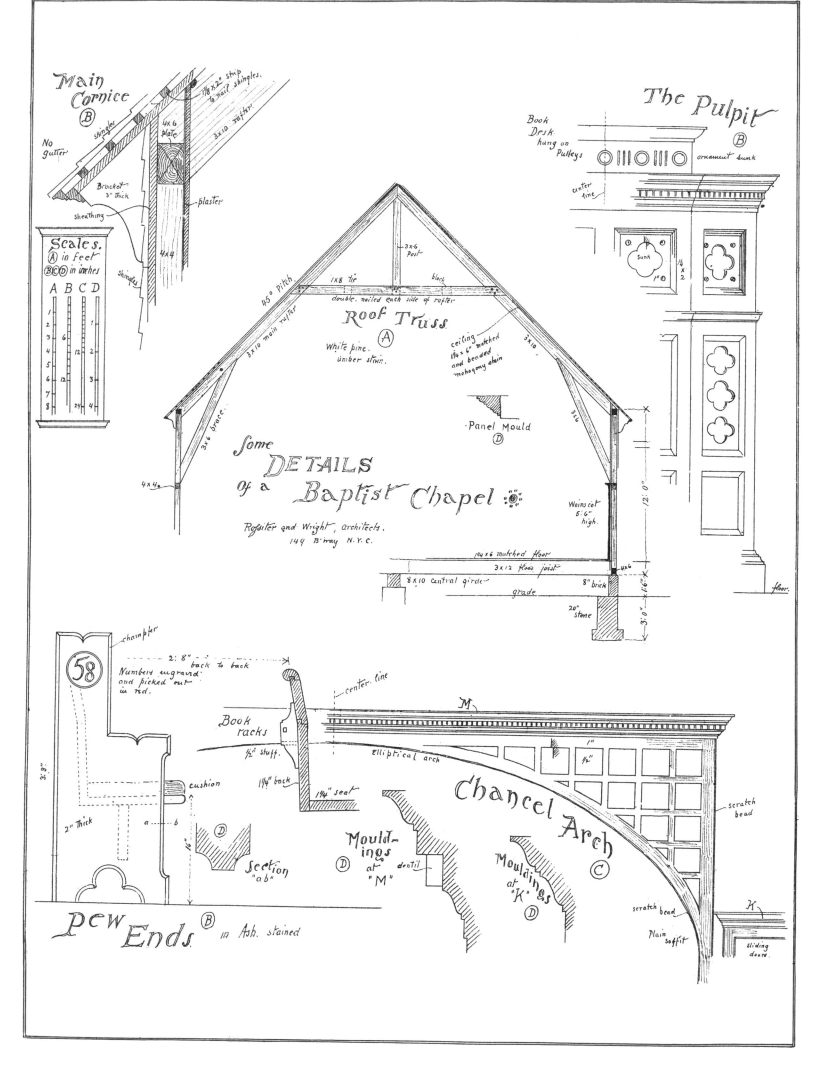

Main Cornice Ⓑ

1⅛" x 2" strip to nail shingles.

No gutter
shingles
4 x 6 plate
3 x 10 rafter
Bracket 3" thick
plaster
Sheathing
shingles
4 x 4

The Pulpit Ⓑ

Book Desk hung on Pulleys
ornament sunk
center line
Sunk
¼ x 2
1" D

Scales.
Ⓐ in feet
ⒷⒸⒹ in inches

A B C D

Roof Truss Ⓐ

3 x 6 Post
1 x 8 tie
block
double, nailed each side of rafter
45° Pitch
3 x 10 main rafter
White pine. umber stain.
ceiling 1¼ x 6" matched and beaded mahogany stain
3 x 10
3 x 6
3 x 6 brace
Panel Mould Ⓓ
4 x 4

Some DETAILS of a Baptist Chapel :❂:

Rossiter and Wright, architects.
149 B'way N.Y.C.

Wainscot 5'-6" high.
12'-0"
1¼ x 6 matched floor
3 x 12 floor joist
4 x 6
8 x 10 central girder
grade
8" brick
floor
3'-0" 1'-6"
20" stone

Pew Ends Ⓑ in Ash. stained

chamfer
58
2'-8" back to back
Numbers engraved and picked out in red.
3'-9"
2" Thick
a   b
Book racks
center line
M
½" stuff
Elliptical arch
1"
½"
1¼" back
1¼" seat
Ⓓ
cushion
Section "ab"
Mouldings at "M" Ⓓ
dentil
Mouldings at "K" Ⓓ
Chancel Arch Ⓒ
scratch bead
scratch bead
Plain soffit
K
sliding doors

SPECIFICATION
—FOR—
LOW-PRICED FRAME COTTAGE.

BY

WM. B. TUTHILL, Architect.

[Refers to Plate XXXII.]

Generally.—All materials shall be the best of their kind specified.

Timber must be clear, sound, true and well-seasoned.

Bricks must be hard burnt, sound and of good shape, laid with close joints struck smooth.

All labor must be thorough.

Measurements.—Measurements marked on the drawings must in all cases be taken in preference to scale measurements.

Laying-out.—The building is to be located on lot as indicated.

Set up batter-boards and line out building accurately. All lengths and angles must be verified before excavation is commenced.

Remove the sod from site of building in as long strips as possible; also all loam. Stack both in a protected place.

Excavations.—Excavate for cellar, foundations of chimney stacks, foundations, areas for cellar windows, steps, drains, cesspool, &c., according to measurements marked on plans and sections. The cellar is to be excavated 8″ deeper than the line of the top of concrete.

All earth from excavations not required for refilling or regrading, is to be carted to such place as may be indicated.

Foundations.—The foundations are to be in all respects according to the drawings. Footings for walls 12″ deep by 30″ wide, of good building stone, in large sizes, laid in cement mortar.

The walls are to be 12″ thick, of hard burnt brick, laid in lime mortar. All joints inside and outside of wall are to be struck smooth.

The foundation posts are to be of straight locust, not less than 5″ in diameter at the smaller end. The larger ends are to be cut true and footed upon pieces of bluestone 3″x14″x14″, set 3′ 6″ or more below ground level.

After brickwork of cellar walls is ready to receive the sill-plate, the heads of all posts are to be cut to a level.

Chimney Stacks.—The chimney stacks are to have a stone footing (of same specification as that for cellar walls), 12″ deep by 4″ larger on all sides than the base of the stack, commenced 4′ 6″ below ground level. Carry up the stacks in hard bricks laid in cement mortar in all respects according to the drawings.

The withs are to be properly bonded with stacks. The topping out of all stacks is to be faced with pressed bricks, laid in cement.

The chimney caps are of red-stone of dimensions given, in one piece and accurately put for the flue openings.

The joints in the flues are to be struck smooth. The flues must be left perfectly clear and clean.

Openings of fire-places in all but main hall, to be furnished with bluestone lintels, 4″x7″x3″ longer on each end than the opening of the fire-place.

Set 6″ cast-iron thimbles where marked.

Turn arches for hearths at all floors.

Fire-place in main hall to have jambs and segmental arch of moulded bricks as per design furnished.

The back of fire-place is to be set with pressed brick. The bottom of fire-place inside of jamb-line is to be laid with pressed brick laid on edge.

Mortar.—Lime mortar to be one part of freshly-burned, thoroughly slaked Rockland lime and two of clean sharp sand.

Cement mortar is to consist of two parts of lime mortar and one of best Rosendale cement.

Concrete.—Lay cellar floor 4″ deep with coarse gravel, well rammed; then lay 4″ of concrete formed of one part of Rosendale cement and two of clean coarse sand.

Hearths.—Hearth in dining-room will be of rubbed bluestone, 1½″ thick, with moulded edges. Level of top of hearth 1″ above level of floor.

Hearth of hall is to be laid with 9 courses of 2½″ Venetian red glazed tiles, and is to have a 3″ beveled cherry border. Level of hearth to be ⅝″ above floor level.

All hearths are to be laid on cement bed. There is no hearth in kitchen.

Plates, &c.—Before the plates are laid, the top of all foundation posts are to be brought to a level with the brickwork of the cellar.

Plates are to be 4″x8″ spruce, notched and spiked upon posts.

The plate on cellar wall is to be well bedded in cement.

Floor Beams.—First and second stories, 3″x8″; set 16″ on centres; ceiling of second story, 2″x8″; set 18″ on centres.

Frame openings for chimney stacks, stair well-holes, &c., as shown in the drawings.

Crossbridging.—Each tier of beams is to be crossbridged every 8 ft. of length (or as marked) with 2″x3″ stuff, accurately cut and firmly nailed.

Frames.—Corner posts, 4″x4″; studs, 3″x4″; set 16″ on centres; interties for second story beams, 2″x6″, mortised into and spiked to studs.

All posts and studs are to be footed directly upon sill plates, and to run through to roof as far as practicable.

Floor beams are to be shouldered upon plates and interties, not more than 1″ of depth. The cutting from the depth of any beam is to be avoided.

Set double studing 2″x4″ at all window and door openings.

Wall plates, 4″x4″, in single lengths when possible, halved and spiked at all angles and joints.

Rafters.—Rafters, 3″x6″; set 20″ on centres for main roofs; 3″x4″ for roofs of porches, &c. All rafters are to be worked where exposed to view, as shown. All rafters are to be firmly spiked to ridge and wall plates. Hip rafters, 3″x9″; ridge, 2″x10″.

Sheathing.—All exterior walls and roofs, except roofs of verandah, are to be sheathed with 9″ hemlock boards (selected), planed on one side to an even thickness, laid diagonally and firmly nailed at every stud. Cover sheathing of walls with one layer of sheathing paper and roof with one layer of roofing felt.

Clapboards, &c.—Clapboard, where marked, with milled boards and firmly nail; show not more than 3½″ face; no joints of the boarding will be allowed in lengths under 16 feet.

Shingles for Roof—All roofs are to be covered with the best sawn cypress shingles, firmly nailed to sheathing; show face of not more than 5″.

Flashings.—Provide and build into chimney stacks counter flashings of 3½ lb. lead. Lay on sheathing wide zinc flashings, which are to be carried close up to chimney and turned up as far as the counter flashing. Then turn down the lead, dress well and solder.

All valleys and hips are to have zinc flashings 12″ wide on each side of valley. Place proper zinc flashings at junction of verandah roof and house wall. Carry up same under clapboards at least 8″.

Partition.—Studs, 3″x4″; set 16″ on centres; sills and caps, 2″x4″. Cut in and firmly nail one course of horizontal bracing, 4′ 6″ above floor line.

Floors.—Lay all floors with 4½″ matched pine flooring, firmly blindnailed at every beam. Each plank must be driven home. Floor in hall is to be laid in selected hard pine. All planks in this floor must be in single lengths.

Windows.—Of dimensions and details shown. Sash, 1½″ thick, of white pine. Sash windows are to be hung on woven hemp sash cord and steel axle pulleys. Provide all sash windows on both stories with fastenings of approved pattern. Casement windows, as marked, are to be hung on plain 3″ butts. They are to be fastened shut with iron bolts and spring catches.

The transoms (which are at the heads of all casement windows, and elsewhere, as indicated) are to be hung on horizontal pivots, so that the head of sash opens inwards, and are to be furnished with spring catches.

All windows, unless otherwise specified, are to be glazed with the best quality double thick, perfectly clear window glass.

The sash of the middle window on front of sitting room is to be glazed with a single sheet of plate glass. The sash is to be fixed.

Stained glass will be inserted where directed, and shall be of kind, quality and design as may be desired by owner.

Gable windows in roof are to be glazed with common glass. The sash are to be hung on strong cast iron butts, so as to open inwards, and are to be fastened shut with iron buttons.

Doors.—All of pine. Exterior, 1¾″ thick ; interior, 1½″ thick ; hung on cast iron butts. Exterior doors are to be finished as per detail. Interior doors are to have four panels, chamfered stiles, stopped mouldings. Such interior doors as are marked to be glazed are to have the upper panels filled with ⅛″ fine ribbed glass, or with stained glass, as may be directed.

The glass for exterior doors (where glazed) is to be perfectly clear, double thick window glass. All doors, except those of closets, are to be furnished with 5½″ brass face mortice locks and proper keys. Main doors (exterior) to have 6″ brass face mortice locks, with one key ; also night latch with 3 keys.

Pantry and closet doors to have 4″ rim locks and keys. All doors to have brass striking-plates. Provide all exterior doors with square flat bolts not less than 4½″ long. Those on doors of hall are to be of brass. All double doors are to be furnished with brass face flush bolts.

The furniture of all doors will be as selected by owner or architect. Roses and escutcheons are to match.

Exterior Finish.—As per drawings. 1st story furnished with clapboards as before specified. False stiles, 1″x4″ wide ; window casings, 1″x4″, with moulded edges. Second story furnished with best pine shingles, cut with circular ends ; shingles to show not more than 5½″ face. Base boards to be of 9″ planks, slotted at joints.

Interior Finish.—All of white pine, except in stair hall and sitting room, where selected California red wood is to be used. Trims, 4″x1″, reeded, with turned corner blocks. All door trims to be carried down to floor. Jambs of doors are to be reeded same as trims. Base, 8″ high, with moulded top, and is to be set before flooring is laid.

Stairs.—To be in all respects according to the plans and details furnished.

Newels, handrail and balusters are to be of red wood. Treads and risers are to be of cherry, ploughed together. Nosing and cove are to be returned on ends of treads and carried around stairwell on second story. On bottom of outside string set mould to cover plaster joint.

Firmly frame stairs, and set on three 3″x10″ carriages. Treads and risers are to be housed into string. Framing of platform 3″x8″. Place base board against wall. The space below stairs is to be panelled in.

All work on stairs is to be executed in the best manner. Hand and base rails are to be housed into newel and corner posts, and balusters accurately morticed and tenoned into rail.

Mantels.—Yellow pine frames and shelves—filled in with unglazed tiles. Fireplaces are to be furnished with a brass frame, and cast iron linings. (See details furnished).

Pantries and Closets.—Provide all pantries with three white pine shelves, 14″ wide ; the lowest shelf to be set 3′ 2″ above floor line. All shelving must be firmly set on cleats nailed to studding. Set in all closets, one shelf 12″ wide, 6′ 4″ above floor line ; also a strip for clothes hooks, 6″ below shelf line and securely fastened to studs. Provide and set at least eight japanned clothes hooks in each closet.

Verandahs.—As per drawings.

Rafters, 3″x6″ ; posts, 4½″x4½″ ; finished as shown. Plates, 4″x4″. Roofs are to be sheathed with 6″ clear matched pine boards, planed on both sides and firmly nailed.

Floor beams, 3″x8″, set 18″ on centre, to rest on plates as indicated. Lay floors with 1″x4½″ hard pine, without tongue and groove, and set ⅜″ apart. Floor to have a wash of 1″ to outside.

Iron Work.—Provide and set wrought iron finials on main ridge, of detail as furnished.

PLUMBING, &c.

Water Closet.—Furnish and set complete with plain cistern, cranks, levers, &c., a (Demarest's " *Whirlpool* ") closet. The work must in all respects be perfect. The seat, cover, panelling, &c., is to be of yellow pine. Frame seat and cover, and hang both on 2″ brass hinge. Front panel is to be held in position by brass buttons.

Sink.—In kitchen, set on strong galvanized iron brackets, an earthenware sink, 20½″x14½″x6″ deep, inside measurement. Set 1½″x3½″ ash frame

on upper edge. Provide and set 2″ waste, " *A* " lead pipe, and S trap. Waste to be connected with sink by proper brass fastenings. To the end of waste solder a brass ferule and caulk into branch from drain.

Set in kitchen where indicated, a Blunt's force pump. (Lotus No. 7.) Make 1″ connection with driven or sunk well (located and built under direction of owner). The pipe must be the best " *A* " pipe, and have a continuous descent to cellar, so that all water may be drained from it in winter. Place a stop cock at the lowest point. From pump carry ⅝″ branch lines to kitchen sink and to tank of closet. Set brass way cock in the pipe, so regulated that of the whole quantity of water pumped, one-third shall go to the water-closet tank, while two-thirds goes to the sink.

Set brass faucet at sink. The pipe and faucet are to be attached to a splash board.

The supply to tank is to enter at top. An overflow is to be provided opening 3″ below top line of tank and carried down wall and empty into bowl of closet.

Waste from water closet, 3″ " *A* " pipe, with S trap, carried in single lengths to drain.

The drain end of waste is to have a brass ferule soldered to it and is to be properly caulked into drain.

On crown of trap attach a 2″ lead pipe, carry up on the outside of house through line of the eaves, and terminate in a short straight length of pipe, about 8″ or 10″ long, without return.

All traps are to be provided with brass trap screws. Vertical pipes must be properly supported by hard metal tucks soldered to pipe and screwed to woodwork. Horizontal pipes must be supported their entire length and fastened by brass bands. All joints in plumbing work are to be thoroughly and properly made, and all material and workmanship must be thorough in every particular.

Drain.—Lay from house to cesspool a 6″ glazed earthen drain, as indicated on plan. It must be laid in a direct and unbroken line, and with a descent to cessposl of not less than 6″ in every 10 feet. All joints must be made with cement, and smoothed on the inside. The pipe must be well bedded throughout its entire length.

Provide and set at house end of drain a return and Y branch for sink and water-closet. From return carry up a 6″ earthen pipe, at least 1′ 0″ above ground level and finish with galvanized iron cowl.

Cesspool.—Is to be located according to the nature of the ground, not less than 50 feet from the nearest point of house. Diameter, 7′ 0″ ; depth, 9′ 0″ : lining, 8″ thick, of hard brick laid in cement. Lay bottom with brick in cement. The top of cesspool is to be arched over, leaving an opening of 2′ 8″ in diameter, which is to be covered with a piece of bluestone 3″ thick. The opening of cesspool is to be not less than 2′ 0″ below ground level. Into top of cesspool set a 6″ earthen ventilation pipe, and carry same at least 16″ above ground and finish with a galvanized iron cowl. The house drain is to project at least 2′ 0″ into cesspool.

Plastering.—Lath walls and ceilings of all rooms, halls, passages, closets, pantries, &c. The lath must be straight, well seasoned, free from knots, and firmly nailed.

Plaster two coats with rough white sand finish. First coat is to be well mixed with hair, which must be properly and sufficiently soaked and beaten before being used.

Carry all coats of plastering close up to line of all openings and down to floor line.

No cornices will be run or centre pieces set.

Painting.—All woodwork on inside and outside is to be properly prepared for painting. All holes must be puttied. The surface of all interior woodwork is to be sandpapered perfectly smooth.

Interior woodwork is to be oiled, two coats of the best raw oil. Let first coat dry thoroughly. The second coat is to be slightly colored by the addition of a small quantity of the best burnt sienna. The oil should be just colored, but should have no body. After second coat is thoroughly dry, apply one coat of white shellac. Outside woodwork, including shingles of roof and sides, is to be painted with at least two coats of the best color ground in linseed oil. The colors to be used will be selected by owner or architect.

Fences.—As per drawings furnished. Posts, 4½″x4½″, locust or chestnut, turned heads, chamfered angles ; set 7′ 0″ between centres, 3′ 6″ in ground, and footed on piece of bluestone, 3″x12″x12″. The posts are to be coated with asphalt to 4 ft. from lower end. They must be set perfectly plumb, and the earth well rammed around them.

Top rail, 2″x4″, moulded ; bottom and mid-rail, 2″x2¾″, with beaded angles ; palings, 1″x1″, plain. All of pine.

All the work is to be done in the most thorough manner.

Gates are to be hung on proper wrought iron hinges, so as to open both ways. Spring catches are to be furnished.

Regrading.—Refill about cellar walls and well ram the earth. Regrade on all sides of house with surface soil, giving a wash away from walls of 10″ in 10 feet.

All parts of the premises that have been in any way disturbed by building operations, must be put in perfect order. Such other regrading as is required, is to be carried out under special directions given at the time.

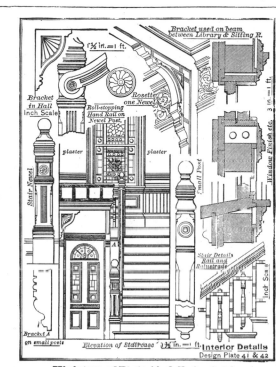

→AN IMPROVED←

ADAPTED TO THE USE OF
Architects, Engineers, Masons, Builders, Farmers and others,

LEVELING INSTRUMENT

This Instrument is made of Brass and Iron, Lacquered and Japanned so that it will not corrode, and consists of the following principal parts:

THE SIGHTING TUBE A A'. THE HORIZONTAL CIRCLE AND THE LOWER DISC OR BASE B.

THE ONLY LOW PRICED LEVEL THAT CAN BE THOROUGHLY ADJUSTED IN THE FIELD

Price of Instrument, Complete,   - - - - $20.00

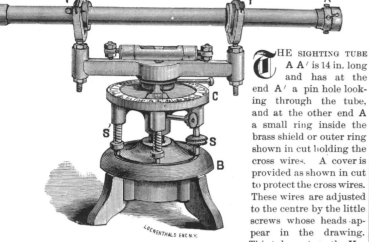

LOEWENTHALS ENC.N.Y.

Description of the Level.

THE SIGHTING TUBE A A' is 14 in. long and has at the end A' a pin hole looking through the tube, and at the other end A a small ring inside the brass shield or outer ring shown in cut holding the cross wires. A cover is provided as shown in cut to protect the cross wires. These wires are adjusted to the centre by the little screws whose heads appear in the drawing. This tube rests in the Ys, Y and Y'. On this tube at the **Ys** are two rings with flanges, like car wheels, and it is held in its place by the latches on the top of the **Ys**. By loosening these latches this sighting tube may be revolved to test the adjustment of the cross wires.

At the feet of the **Ys** will be seen the nuts, one above and one below the end of the cross bar, which may be turned, thus raising or lowering the end of the tube and adjusting the line of sight to the line of level. The circle C is graduated to 10° and the pointer marked to degrees, so that the instrument may be used in laying off angles, squaring foundations, &c. The pointer is movable and can be fixed in position by the set screw shown in the cut just below the cross bar. It is usual to set the pointer to O in starting any work, which is done as follows : by means of the set screw beneath the circle, fix the instrument when looking toward first station so that it will not revolve on its axis, then loosen up the clamp of the pointer so it may be revolved, and bring it to O and clamp it firmly there, then loosen the set screw beneath the circle and the instrument is ready for use. The cross bar carries the glass bubble which is seen in the cut. The bubble itself may be adjusted by the screws. In the centre of this cross bar will be seen the head of axis about which the circles revolve. To the circle are attached the two thumb screws and springs opposite to them by means of which the instrument is brought to a level.

In the outer edge of the Base B is a smoothly turned groove in which the feet of the screws and springs may slip easily whenever it may be necessary to revolve the circle on the base. The centre of the base is formed into a socket for the ball referred to above. The under surface has a solid cylinder which screws in the collar of the tripod. The cord suspending the plumb-bob drops from the centre of the instrument to which it is attached by a loop not shown in the cut. From this description it will be seen that this instrument can be *adjusted* in every way possible in the highest priced instruments, and has besides the additional feature of a horizontal circle, making it in reality a plain transit, as well as level.

To ADJUST THE LEVEL.—This operation requires a little patience, but when understood is easily accomplished. There are three adjustments :—

1st. To bring the level tube or bubble parallel to the plane of the circle C. 2d. That of the cross wires. 3d. That of the **Ys** or to bring the line of the sight parallel to the line of the circle, so that when the circle is level the line of sight is horizontal.

The first adjustment is made as follows :   Bring the **Ys** over one of the screws S and its opposite spring S' and level up with the screw until the bubble appears in the centre, then reverse the plate, noticing where the bubble settles, and if it does not remain at the centre by means of the screws at the ends of the cradle bring it half way from its present position to the centre, then level up again by means of the screw S. and then reverse. If it then varies from the centre, repeat the same operation, dividing the distance until it appears in the centre every time, when it will be level.

2d. Adjustment, that of the cross wires. Loosen up the catches on top of the **Ys**, then look through the tube toward some perpendicular object, and bring the perpendicular wire in line with such object, then turn the tube half way round, and if the cross wire varies from the object, move it by means of the screws at A half the distance, then revolve the tube back to its first position, and if it then varies, halve the difference again, repeating the process until the wire touches the perpendicular line of the object in both positions of the tube, then revolve the tube one-quarter and repeat the operation with the horizontal cross wire until it lines with the object, when the intersection of the cross wires should be in the centre. To test this more fully, while looking through the tube notice the point at which the intersection of the cross wires touch the object, and revolve the tube slowly in the Ys, and if it is in the centre it will not move from this point, otherwise it will describe a circle one side of which contains the point, in which case it is to be further adjusted until there is no variation from this point.

The 3d adjustment, that of the **Ys**, is accomplished by the raising or lowering the **Ys**, by means of the nuts above and below the cross bar. This adjustment may be made in several ways : where you have two points you know to be on a dead level, set your instrument where it will look over them and sight across them, and if the intersection of the cross wires strikes both these points or an equal distance above or below them, the line of sight is horizontal or parallel to the plane of the circle, if not it must be raised or lowered until it is. A second method is to set the instrument and measure off equal distances on either side of it, and take the height where it strikes at either station and then move the instrument to a third station an equal distance, and in a line with the two stations, and if it then strikes the marks fixed by the two preceding observations or equal distances above or below, it is level, otherwise it must be adjusted until it does. A third method is, where you are near a still body of water, drive several stakes so that their tops come just even with the top of the water, and try them, and if the cross wires mark equal distances above them all, the instrument is level, otherwise it must be adjusted until it comes to the same height above each. This last method supposes great care to be taken in driving the stakes and that the sights are taken at long distance. *Every instrument will be fully adjusted before it is shipped.*

The instrument is put up in a handsome wooden box with strap for carrying and furnished with a surveyor's tripod and a short or mason's tripod.

Price of Instrument, complete, $20.

Forwarded by express on receipt of price. The charges of transportation from New York to the purchaser are in all cases to be borne by him, I guaranteeing the safe arrival of all instruments to the extent of express transportations, and holding the express companies responsible to me for all losses or damages on the way.

A NEW LEVELING ROD.

This rod is round and made in two sections, so that it can be conveniently carried, is united by a solid screw joint, so that when together it is as firm as if of one length and has a target as shown in illustration, made to slide on the rod.

There are two scales : one side being Engineer's (feet, 10ths and 100ths) ; the other Architects' scale (or, feet, inches and 8ths). This rod will be found by engineers light and convenient, and well worth its price as a second rod where they have one of the ordinary make. To architects and builders it will be invaluable, as it gives them the measurements in feet and inches.

Forwarded by express on receipt of price. The charges of transportation from New York to the purchaser are in all cases to be borne by him.

Price, - - - - - - - - - $6.00

Where the Level is ordered with the rod. the price of the two will be, . **$25.00**

WILLIAM T. COMSTOCK, Manufacturer,

6 ASTOR PLACE, NEW YORK.